The Mafia and Politics:
The Italian State Under Siege

Judith Chubb

Western Societies Program
Occasional Paper No. 23
Center for International Studies
Cornell University

© Copyright Judith Chubb 1989

CONTENTS

The Italian State Under Siege

In the 1970s and the 1980s the Italian state came under direct and violent attack on two fronts: terrorism and the mafia. By the early 1980s the left-wing terrorism of the Red Brigades had been isolated and defeated by an increasingly efficient police operation backed up by a broad coalition of political and social forces in defense of democratic institutions. In contrast, the struggle of the Italian state against the mafia continues to be characterized by a strikingly lower level of commitment not only in term of men and means but, most importantly, in terms of political support. How can the very different behavior of the Italian state in response to these two quite distinct, but equally deadly, attacks on its representatives and its institutions be explained? This monograph will argue that the key to understanding the distinctive nature of the mafia lies precisely in its relationship to political power and political institutions. Even at its height terrorism remained essentially an external enemy, politically isolated, and after the assassination of Aldo Moro in 1978, increasingly deprived of even the limited social support it had initially enjoyed among some sectors of intellectuals, disaffected youth, and the working class and undermined by growing defections among its own ranks.

The relationship of the mafia to dominant elites and institutions is quite a different one. The difficulty of the Italian state in combatting the mafia arises fundamentally from the fact that the mafia is not, like terrorism, an external enemy but rather one which has succeeded in penetrating deeply into the very institutions which are supposed to be fighting it. It is this presence of the mafia within the very structure of the Italian state which renders it a much more insidious and ultimately a much more dangerous threat to democratic institutions than was the more openly subversive but more vulnerable and exposed phenomenon of left-wing terrorism.

In order to understand the nature of the threat which the mafia poses to the contemporary Italian state, it is necessary first to analyze the nature and functions of the traditional agrarian mafia and then to examine the transformations that took place from the

1

mid-1950s on both in the socio-economic functions of the mafia and in its relationship to political power. This monograph will base its analysis on the Sicilian mafia as it has evolved from Italian unification in 1860 to the present. Although other forms of organized crime in southern Italy (like the Neapolitan *camorra* and the Calabrian *'ndrangheta*) have achieved notoriety, their origins are quite distinct. Not only is the Sicilian mafia much better documented; most importantly, it presents in a much sharper form those characteristics which distinguish "mafia" from other forms of criminal behavior—in particular its organic relationship with the political system. It is only in recent years, as a process of inter-penetration and homogenization of these three forms of organized crime has taken place, that it makes sense to think of them as parts of a single phenomenon.[1]

The Traditional Mafia: The "Man of Honor"

As a point of departure it is essential to define what is intended by the term "mafia" and to make clear those features which distinguish "mafia" from other forms of criminal activity. First, the term "mafia" as used in this article does *not* refer to a secret and unified criminal society, with rites of initiation, statutes, and a hierarchical chain of command linking each level of the pyramid to the one below it. The issue of the organizational structure of the mafia has long constituted an important point of debate among scholars and publicists. Popular literature has tended to present a picture of the mafia as a tightly organized criminal association. Scholars, on the other hand, have argued that such a conception of the Mafia (with a capital "M") represents a distortion of reality; studies of the traditional agrarian mafia have used the term "mafia" to refer not to a formal criminal association, but rather to the sum of the activities of individuals and groups whose mode of behavior rather than their membership in a secret criminal society is what defines them as *mafioso*. The obvious parallels among the activities of various *mafiosi* are seen as reflecting not the existence of a central headquarters coordinating the activities of a far-flung criminal empire, but instead a fundamental identity in the values, in the goals pursued, and in the social functions performed by each

2

mafia boss and his subordinates in each local setting. Although the single mafia family or *cosca* is strongly centralized, this takes the form of a series of diadic relationships between the *capo-mafia* and each of the individual members. The mafia as a whole is thus seen as a complex of social networks, held together by traditional bonds of honor, kinship and "instrumental friendship."[2] Typically the activities of the *cosca* are limited to a well-defined territory, over which it enjoys a monopoly of protection and control. To the extent that a structure going beyond the *cosca* exists, it is a loose "federal" structure in which each *cosca*, autonomous in its own territorial or sectoral sphere of influence, enters into alliances or coalitions with its neighbors in the pursuit of larger-scale economic interests.[3]

However, the judicial investigations preceding the opening of the major mafia trial in Palermo in 1986 reopened the debate over the organizational structure of the mafia. In their preparatory documents, the Palermo magistrates argued that, as a result of the large-scale entrance of the mafia into the international drug trade, the organizational structure of the mafia has been revolutionized. Traditional "family" and territorial structures, no longer adequate for the scale of the economic transactions involved, have been replaced by a tightly centralized, unitary organization, corresponding quite closely to popular images of a secret criminal society. Individual families have become non-autonomous units in a large bureaucratic whole, with all major decisions being made by a single ruling "Cupola" or "Commission" (Stajano 38-63). A closer look at the evidence, however, suggests that such a conclusion may represent an oversimplification. The Palermo trial evidence itself documents alternate phases of the constitution and breakdown of the Commission, of coordination and of conflict, the latter exemplified most recently by the unprecedented violence of a bloody intra-mafia war for supremacy during the early 1980s (although this pattern of alternation between a relatively stable *pax mafiosa* and violent competition among and within families recurs throughout the history of the mafia). Because of the highly personalistic nature of mafia power, founded on the fear and respect inspired by the single *capo-mafia*, there is never a stable passage to forms of peaceful competition; violence remains the

3

ultimate source of power, with new contenders constantly emerging to challenge the institutionalization of the status quo imposed by the dominant groups. This suggests that a more accurate image of the contemporary mafia might be that of a confederation of competing sovereign states which have entered into a mutual security arrangement in order to pursue affairs in their reciprocal self-interest. What we see, then, is not a unified organization, but rather a system of shifting alliances based on changes in the relative balance of power among the various families or coalitions. While there is an interest in maintaining a higher body in order to regulate competition and limit destructive conflicts, the intense rivalry among the component groups, given the magnitude of the interests at stake, periodically becomes so intense as to break down the organizational arrangements intended to confine it, leading to unrestrained warfare like that which wracked metropolitan areas like Palermo and Naples in the first half of the 1980s.[4] It could also be argued that, despite tremendous changes in the nature and scope of mafia activities, the territorial base of mafia families remains an important element in their success, creating a foundation of social support in areas where a dominant "criminal subculture" has come to predominate, providing protection for certain illegal activities (e.g., contraband, extortion, drug refining), and constituting the basis for solid linkages to the institutions of local government.

A second analytical problem is that of distinguishing "mafia" from other forms of criminal behavior. Very briefly, the following traits have historically demarcated the mafia from mere corruption on the one hand and from other forms of delinquency on the other: (1) the use of violence or the threat of violence to acquire illicit gains and to build up and maintain a position as a "man of honor;" (2) the existence of a broad base of social support and legitimation—within the local community the *mafioso* is not branded as a criminal, but is rather regarded as a leader, admired and respected as well as feared; (3) organic linkages with the political system—the development of a network of political ties that allow the *mafioso* and the interests he represents to penetrate deeply into legitimate institutions and that guarantee him immunity from prosecution. These traits apply most fully to the traditional mafia as it develop-

4

ed in central and western Sicily in the period between 1860 and the mid-1950s. The mafia of the 1980s differs in some important respects from the model set out above. These changes can be traced to the breakdown from the mid-1950s on of the traditional agrarian mafia and of the cultural and socio-economic context which sustained it. The profound transformations in the nature and role of the mafia from the 1950s to the present will be discussed in the second part of this monograph.

A central focus of much of the literature on the mafia, both scholarly and popular, has been the existence of a set of traditional subcultural norms which have, as noted above, created a basis of social support for the mafia which distinguish it from other forms of criminal activity. In a classic inquiry into the social, economic, and political conditions of Sicily carried out for the Italian Parliament in 1875, Leopoldo Franchetti and Sidney Sonnino emphasized that the power of the mafia was based not so much on fear as on moral authority, rooted in the mafia's congruence with the dominant cultural norms of Sicilian society (Franchetti and Sonnino 127-128). These norms revolved about the pursuit of honor and the legitimacy of individual violence as a means for attaining it. In this sense, many observers have seen "mafia" as a set of positive attributes deeply rooted in popular culture, as illustrated in the following definition by the eminent Sicilian ethnographer, Giuseppe Pitrè, at the end of the 19th century:

> Mafia is the consciousness of one's own worth,
> the exaggerated concept of individual force as
> the sole arbiter of every conflict, of every clash
> of interests or ideas (Pitrè 289; cited in Hess 1-
> 6-17).

A similar definition of the mafia was voiced by Vittorio Emanuele Orlando, parliamentary deputy from western Sicily and Prime Minister from 1917-1919, who owed his own political success in large part to mafia support. Questioned about the criminal activities of the mafia, Orlando denied that the mafia as a criminal phenomenon existed. Instead, he equated the mafia with all that was best in Sicilian culture:

> if for mafia one intends the sense of honor

carried to the extreme, intolerance for every form of arrogance and intimidation, generosity that confronts the strong but indulges the weak, loyalty to friendships; if for mafia one intends these sentiments and attitudes, then in this sense they are individual manifestations of the Sicilian soul, and I declare myself *mafioso* and am proud to do so (cited in Antimafia Commission 1972, Vol. 1: 267).

Franchetti and Sonnino noted that in Sicily violent actions carried with them no stigma of immorality, that might was accepted as the criterion of right. This they linked to the personalistic basis of Sicilian society:

There is absent in the majority of Sicilians the sentiment of the law as being above all and equal for all... .The personal bond is the only one they understand... .Thus, in Sicilian society, all relationships are based on the concept of individual interests...to the exclusion of any social or public interest (Franchetti and Sonnino 36).

The same principle is embodied in a Sicilian proverb: "Cu dinari e cu amicizia, 'nculu a giustizia" ("With money and with friendship, you can screw justice"). The clearest expression of this disregard for the law and the dependence on private forms of power and justice is the principle of *omertà* or silence, the refusal to cooperate with legal authorities in the pursuit of someone accused of a criminal action. Again, the point is succinctly made in a popular Sicilian proverb: "Cu e surdu, orbu e taci, campa cent'anni 'mpaci" (He who is deaf, blind and silent will live a hundred years in peace").

Students of the mafia debate whether *omertà* should best be understood as an expression of social consensus surrounding the mafia or whether it is instead a pragmatic response based primarily on fear. While the "mafia spirit" described above may have developed over the centuries in Sicily as an expression of revolt against outside domination, it developed after 1860 into a "Sicilianist" ideology, a rhetoric of self-justification against the Italian state and against outsiders who identified the source of Sicily's ills in presumed flaws of the Sicilian character. The Sicilianist ideology reacted against such accusations by exalting (like Pitrè and Orlando) the Sicilian code of honor, identifying the mafia with broader subcultural values, and thereby denying its existence as a distinct criminal phenomenon. Pre-existing cultural codes were thus manipulated in a self-serving fashion by the mafia itself to justify its existence and obscure its ultimate reliance on violence and intimidation and by local elites to deflect attention from their own complicity.

It is a mistake in any case to see the mafia purely as an expression of the Sicilian character or of pre-modern cultural values. To understand the development of the mafia in the 19th and 20th centuries, it is necessary to place the mafia in the context of the economic, social and political arrangements within which it emerged and thrived. Recent scholarly analyses of the origins of the mafia depict it not as a residue of a feudal past, but rather as a product of the disintegration of the feudal system and the penetration of the market and the modern state into the Sicilian countryside in the 19th century—a situation of transition in which traditional relationships of economic and political power were breaking down but not fully replaced by the impersonal structures of the market and the state.[5] These processes were set into motion by the attempts of the Bourbon rulers of the Kingdom of the Two Sicilies beginning in the 1820s to undermine the feudal structure of landownership and the power of the barons by passing reforms intended to encourage the creation of a new class of smallholders.[6] This process of breaking up the vast feudal estates or *latifondi* was continued after the unification of Italy, in 1860, through the sale of Church and communal lands. Unlike the rest of southern Italy, however, the process of breaking up the feudal estates proceeded much more slowly in Sicily and with consequences quite different from the original intention of creating a smallholding peasant class. Land did change hands, but the structure of land tenancy was not significantly altered; in fact, with the sale of Church and demanial lands, the weight of large-scale private property further increased. The main effect of the reforms was to create a new bourgeois landowning class (a prototype of which is found in the character of Don Calogero Sedara in Giuseppe

7

Tomasi di Lampedusa's novel, *The Leopard*) alongside the landed aristocracy while further increasing the number of landless peasants and the pressure of population upon the remaining available land. This rising bourgeoisie perpetuated a semi-feudal relationship between the landed elite and the peasantry. Thus, despite the destruction of the legal basis of feudalism and the emergence of a new landowning bourgeoisie, the *latifondo* as an economic and social system continued to dominate central and western Sicily until the end of the Second World War.

The 19th and 20th century *latifondo* system which prevailed in the interior of central and western Sicily has been described as a form of "rent capitalism" specialized in the production and export of grain for international markets and profitable as a result of exploitation of land and labor rather than of productive investment in the agricultural process.[7] Most of the landowning elite, both aristocratic and bourgeois, preferred life in the great urban centers of Palermo or Naples to existence in the desolate Sicilian countryside. The large estates were leased out to long-term tenants or *gabelloti*, who ran the estates in the owners' absence, dividing them into smaller plots for sublet to peasant sharecroppers. These "rural entrepreneurs" thus effectively controlled the livelihood of the peasants, who depended upon them for access to the land and who, given the pressure of overpopulation and the scarcity of available land, could be squeezed to the limit of survival. At the same time they accumulated wealth as well at the expense of the absentee landlords whom they cheated at the other end and who, finding themselves in financial difficulties, could often be persuaded to sell off parts of their estates at advantageous prices. Many mafia bosses began their careers as poor peasants or shepherds, then, having distinguished themselves by their capacity for violence and *prepotenza* (the rule of the strongest), became *gabelloti* on large estates and eventually landowners in their own right. In addition to land ownership, many *mafiosi* also became involved in the transformation and commercialization of agricultural products, as well as illegal activities such as cattle rustling, and acquired a leading role in rural banks and cooperatives, thereby reinforcing their position as privileged intermediaries in the economic transactions between the village and the larger society.[8]

The mafia thus emerged in response to the breakup of the feudal system and the increased possibilities for entrepreneurship and upward mobility which that breakup engendered.[9] With the abolition of feudalism,

> both wealth and the capacity to prevail through violence became accessible to a larger number of people, and the ruffians, who before had been in the employ of the barons, became independent; thus, to obtain their services, they now had to be dealt with as equals... .

> the industry of violence [thus] came to have an independent existence and organization... .[In Sicily] the criminal class is in a special situation, one that bears no resemblance to that of delinquents in other countries, no matter how numerous, intelligent, and well organized. One could almost say that it has become a social institution. In addition to serving the interests of pre-existing social forces [i.e., the absentee landowners], it has become, as a result of the special conditions brought about by the new order, a class with its own interests and industry, a social force in and of itself (Franchetti and Sonnino 72, 90-91).

√The *mafioso* can thus best be understood, in the words of Anton Blok, as a "violent peasant entrepreneur," specializing in a role of economic and political mediation between traditional social classes and between the countryside and the outside world. One of the most acute students of the traditional mafia, Blok defines the *mafioso* as a "political middleman or power broker, whose raison d'être lies in his capacity to acquire and maintain control over the paths linking the local infrastructure of the village to the superstructure of the larger society" (Blok 7). He plays a key role in managing the processes of conflict and accommodation among the state, the landowning elite, and the peasants, as well as monopolizing the critical junctures between the countryside and the larger economic and political systems.

9

First of all, the *mafioso* performed functions of economic inter-mediation. In the course of the nineteenth century, *mafiosi*, through the exercise or threat of violence, came to hold monopoly positions in a series of markets, both legal and illegal. In the countryside, through their position as *gabelloti*, they controlled access to the key resource, the land, managing the gap between the peasants and the absentee landowning class, and between production and commercialization of the main crop, grain, which was transported to and sold in urban markets through networks monopolized by *mafiosi*. In addition to such intermediation in legal transactions, the mafia also organized its own illegal ac-tivities, the most prominent being protection rackets and the entire cycle of animal rustling, clandestine butchering, and the transport of the meat to urban markets.

While most studies of the traditional mafia have focussed on the interior latifundial zones of central and western Sicily, it is impor-tant to note that the mafia was from the outset an urban as well as a rural phenomenon. In fact, early accounts of the mafia em-phasize its presence not in the *latifondo* but in the intensive agriculture (primarily citrus groves) of the fertile and prosperous coastal plain (the Conca d'Oro) surrounding the city of Paler-mo—both before and after Unification the center of economic and political power in Sicily. The historian Pasquale Villari wrote in 1875,

> the largest number of crimes are committed by the inhabitants of the outskirts of Palermo, who are not poor, but instead often property-owning peasants successfully cultivating their orchards of oranges. In the Conca d'Oro agriculture pros-pers; large-scale property does not exist; the peasant is well off, *mafioso*, and commits a large number of crimes (Villari 55-56).

It is probably most accurate, then, to see the mafia not as a product of backwardness but of possibilities of enrichment and mobility, not of the *latifondo* system alone but of the relationship *between* the city of Palermo and its agricultural hinterland, be it the desolate expanses of the interior or the flourishing orchards of the Conca d'Oro (Catanzaro 1988: 20-24, 109-116; Lupo). In the rich and diversified agricultural economy of the coast, the foundation of mafia power lay in the institution of *guardiania*, a system of oversight and protection of the citrus groves similar to that provided by the *gabelloto* in the countryside. As in the countryside, this also placed the mafia in a crucial position in the marketing of the produce, the wholesale markets of Palermo being cited already in reports of the 1860s and 1870s as bastions of mafia power. Finally, in addition to controlling transportation and commercial networks, *mafiosi* also monopolized the supply of irrigation water critical to the success of the coastal agriculture and owned many of the mills and presses for grain, wine and olive oil.

Some scholars have suggested that the distinguishing characteristic of the *mafioso* is that he is a vendor of *trust*—utilizing subcultural values of honor, instrumental friendship, and the legitimacy of private violence to guarantee stable economic transactions in a fragmented and highly competitive market situation characterized by the absence of the impersonal contractual or legal guarantees of the fully developed capitalist market and modern state (Catanzaro 1985: 38-41; Gambetta; Lupo 479; Schneider and Schneider 107-109). But the *mafioso* was more than a middleman regulating the interactions among distinct economic actors and markets. Through the use or threat of violence, he established and maintained monopoly positions in both legal and illegal economic ventures of his own, often moving back and forth between the legal and illegal sectors. What distinguishes the *mafioso* from other forms of entrepreneurship is the ultimate recourse to violence as a means of regulating competition and of acquiring both social status and wealth—a kind of "primitive accumulation" which will be utilized in the post-World War Two period to launch the mafia into new and even more lucrative economic activities.

The economic bases of mafia power are reflected in its social composition. The sources are not unanimous as to the class basis of the mafia. While some observers have argued that *mafiosi* are to be found among all social classes, others have argued that the mafia is above all a middle-class phenomenon (see Catanzaro 1988: 16-19; Lupo 476). The latter explanation is the more persuasive. Examination of its key economic, social, and political functions shows the mafia to be positioned strategically *between* the peasants and the traditional landed aristocracy. The peasants were most often either the instruments or victims of the mafia, and the large landowners its accomplices or protectors. The mafia in the strict sense, however, was characterized already by Franchetti and Sonnino in their 1875 inquiry as "ruffians of the middle class":

> In Palermo and its hinterland the industry of violence is above all in the hands of members of the middle class. In general this class is considered an element of order and security, especially where it is numerous, as is the case in Palermo... . But this is only an apparent contradiction. In fact, where the middle class does not have the size and influence to insure the dominance of the law over private power, it no longer views the rule of law as a means to conserve its property and status... . Thus when, due to social conditions on the one hand and the impotence of the authorities on the other, the risk of using violence is not greater than that of not using it, any reason for the members of the middle class to sustain law and order ceases (Franchetti and Sonnino 97).

This middle-class status is reflected in the professions typical of *mafiosi*. In the countryside and in the semi-rural towns and villages of the Conca d'Oro, *mafiosi*, while often of peasant origin, rose to become estate guards, *gabelloti* and eventually landowners in their own right. Other typical professions were muleteers and carters (eventually mechanized transport firms), animal herders, wholesale and retail merchants, as well as middle-class professions such as doctors, lawyers, and pharmacists.

Not only was the *gabelloto cum mafioso* a "violent entrepreneur" and a broker between the local economy and external markets; he performed important social and political functions as well.[10] Critical to the emergence and persistence of the mafia was the absence of effective state power in the Sicilian countryside under both the Bourbons and the unified Kingdom of Italy. Except for

12

the tax collector and the conscription officer, the state was distant and was viewed less as a legitimate source of authority than as a hostile and alien occupying force. In the vast empty expanses of the Sicilian countryside, the state as a guarantor of law and order simply did not exist. Thus, in the absence of one of the fundamental defining characteristics of the modern state—the territorial monopoly over the legitimate use of physical violence—private forms of violence and justice filled the gap. In such a context, it was not surprising that the abstract rule of law should carry little weight when confronted with quite concrete and immediate forms of power and coercion or that *omertá*, seen by many outsiders as a tragic flaw of the Sicilian character, should prevail as a rational response to the total inability of legal institutions to provide protection and redress.

In the absence of state power, a kind of Hobbesian universe was created where individual violence and *prepotenza* reigned and gained greater popular legitimacy than the formal institutions of the state. The predominance of informal mechanisms of power and influence like the mafia was reinforced by the terms upon which Italian Unification took place. The relationship between the newly created Kingdom of Italy and the Italian South is the key to understanding the central role played by the mafia in Sicilian society and politics after 1860. It is precisely the relationship of the mafia to political institutions and the legitimacy that the mafia acquired through that relationship which most clearly distinguish the mafia from other forms of delinquency (e.g., banditry) and organized crime. Unification was based upon a tacit alliance between the northern industrial bourgeoisie and the southern landed elite, an alliance which shaped the fundamental outlines of the Italian political system until the Fascist takeover in 1922. The terms of this alliance were perpetuation of the social and economic status quo in the South, complete freedom of action for dominant elites at the local level, and access to government patronage by southern deputies in return for their unquestioning support in Parliament for any government majority, regardless of its program. Such an alliance removed the central government as a meaningful political actor at the local level at the same time as, through the institution of elections and the gradual extension of

13

the suffrage,[11] it greatly strengthened both the autonomy and the national political leverage of local influence brokers. Thus, the new Italian state formally proclaimed a monopoly of violence, but at the same time delegated to local elites the power to govern in its name—those same local elites who were either the perpetrators or the protectors of the system of private violence which ruled de facto in the place of the state.

Given the physical absence of both the central state and of much of the propertied class from the countryside, the local elite came in many cases either to be identical with the mafia or, at the very least, to protect it. In this context, these "violent peasant entrepreneurs" assumed a series of essential functions in social and political life. One set of functions revolved about the maintenance of order and social stability in the countryside. One form this took was "protection"—in return for the payment of tribute—of life and property against attack by thieves or bandits. Although, given the endemic insecurity of the countryside and the inability of the state to provide its own form of protection, such a service was certainly necessary, in reality it was often an extortion racket in which the mafia skimmed a profit off peasant and large landowner alike. If anyone refused to come to terms with the local *capo-mafia*, he would soon find himself subject to thefts, fires, and destruction of property until he saw fit to pay for the necessary "protection."

While protection rackets placed the mafia in a ambiguous position vis-à-vis the dominant classes, other aspects of their social role placed *mafiosi* more squarely on the side of the established order. As we have seen above, central to the *mafioso*'s raison d'être was his role as mediator—not just in the relations between the village and the outside world, but also with regard to conflicts within the local society. In a Hobbesian universe where an intense and unbounded competition for individual honor and wealth would otherwise prevail, the *mafioso*, once having achieved a position of prestige through violence and aggression, then began to seek ways to regulate the intense war of all against all, which would otherwise tear the society apart and threaten his own position. As Calogero Vizzini, one of the last of the "old-style" bosses put it,

The fact is that in every society there has to be a category of people who straighten things out when situations get complicated. Usually they are functionaries of the state. Where the state is not present, or where it does not have sufficient force, this is done by private individuals" (*Corriere della Sera*, October 30, 1949).

In addition to the typical conflicts concerning land rights, debts, the honor of women, and the like, one form of intervention in which the mafia was particularly successful was the restoration of stolen property. In the exercise of this function the mafia proved much more efficient than the police. Some interesting data in this regard were reported by the Fascist Prefect of Palermo, Cesare Mori. According to Mori, in 75% of thefts in his district the official authorities failed to achieve any result; in 15% of the cases they succeeded in finding the guilty party; in only 10% of the cases did they also recover the stolen goods. By contrast, still according to Mori, in 95% of the cases the mediation of the mafia met with full success (data cited in Arlacchi 1986: 24).

A final aspect of the mafia's role as guarantor of order and social stability regards the repression of both common crime and political deviance. In effect, the central government delegated to the mafia the function of maintaining public order in the territories under its control. In this role the mafia became not so much an enemy as a collaborator of the state. It is in this face of the mafia as a guarantor of public order and social peace which illustrates most clearly the contrast with other endemic forms of delinquency such as banditry. The bandit or brigand was a marginal figure, in constant and open conflict with both the state and the dominant classes. The mafia, on the other hand, was at the same time both a competitor and a collaborator of the state and the dominant elite, seeking to preserve and profit by existing structures of power rather than rebelling against them. It is precisely in this ambiguity that the uniqueness of the mafia as a social and political phenomenon lies.

Not only did the mafia effectively curb banditry and common crime in areas under its control; it also served when necessary as the armed agent of the state in the repression of political deviation. Although this face of mafia power emerged as early as the 1890s in response to the formation of the *Fasci Siciliani* (a socialist reform movement), it assumed its most virulent form in the immediate post-World War II period. The period from 1943 to 1950 in Sicily was marked by widespread peasant unrest and mass occupations of large estates, led primarily by the Communist and Socialist parties, in order to put pressure on the government to enact land reform.[12] This mobilization of the peasants helped the Left to win a plurality of the vote in the first elections for the Sicilian regional assembly held in April 1947. During this period the mafia, allied initially with the Sicilian Separatist Movement (dominated by the large landowners fearful of left-wing influence at the national level) brought many bandits into the Separatist "army" to be used as front-line troops against the peasant movement and the left-wing parties.[13] The threat posed to the traditional social order by large-scale peasant mobilization, combined with the broader international context of increasing Cold War tensions, led as well to contacts with representatives of the Christian Democratic Party, already emerging as the dominant political force at both the regional and national levels. An exemplary illustration of the way in which the mafia used bandits to serve its own ends, as well as broader political interests, is the case of Salvador Giuliano.[14] Initially an enemy of the great landowners and the mafia in the tradition of the southern Italian brigand, Giuliano was coopted by the mafia to terrorize the peasants who were organizing to occupy the great estates. On May 1, 1947, two weeks after the electoral victory of the Left, Giuliano's band attacked a peaceful gathering of peasants celebrating Labor Day outside the town of Portella delle Ginestre, leaving 11 dead and 56 wounded. The massacre at Portella delle Ginestre marked the peak of a campaign of terror in which the mafia, either directly or through intermediaries like Giuliano, assassinated scores of peasant leaders and trade-union organizers.[15] This campaign of violence and intimidation successfully decapitated the peasant movement and seriously undermined the electoral base of the left-wing parties. When Giuliano's usefulness had been exhausted, however, and he threatened to become politically dangerous, he was in turn eliminated through a joint effort of the mafia and the *carabinieri*—testimony once again to the ambiguous relationship between private and official violence. During the 1951 trial of the surviving members of Giuliano's band for the deaths at Portella delle Ginestre, the role played by the mafia and national political leaders emerged clearly; as Giuliano's lieutenant, Gaspare Pisciotta, announced at the trial, "We are a single body—bandits, police, and mafia—like the Father, Son, and Holy Ghost" (Antimafia Commission 1976: 131). However, no judicial action was taken against those to whom the finger of political responsibility pointed. As for Pisciotta, who swore that he would eventually reveal the truth about those responsible for the crimes committed by Giuliano and his band, he died a suspicious death of poisoning inside the high-security prison of Palermo.

The political role of the mafia, however, went beyond the maintenance of order in the countryside and the repression of political deviance through violence and intimidation. It also served the critical function of *political* mediation, linking the local society to broader structures of political consensus and democratic representation. In a situation where politics was dominated by personalistic ties, where neither mass parties nor broader structures of interest representation had penetrated, *mafiosi*, as the holders of significant positions of local influence, quickly became great electors, mobilizing support for candidates in both local and national elections or, in some cases, went beyond the function of brokerage to assume local elective positions in their own right. As Franchetti and Sonnino put it in their 1875 report on conditions in Sicily, "The primary responsibility for the disorder in many local administrations lies with the mafia, which has penetrated all the parties and prospers there at the expense of the public interest" (Franchetti and Sonnino xxv).[16] In a similar vein and in the same year, the magistrate Diego Tajani proclaimed in a speech to the Chamber of Deputies, "The mafia ... is not dangerous or invincible in and of itself, but because it is an instrument of local government" (cited in Catanzaro 1988: 109). This direct link to the institutions of local government gave the mafia access to public funds and to a wide range of patronage resources which allowed it to further consolidate its wealth and power and its hold over the local population. In addition, because of its control of many local

17

administrations and its crucial role in the election of many parliamentary deputies, the mafia in turn received protection, recognition, and legitimation from national authorities.[17] In the words of the Sicilian historian, Francesco Renda, what distinguishes the mafia from other forms of delinquency is that "it commits crimes with the almost total certainty of impunity from justice, being able to count on complicity, connivance and support in order to throw sand into the machine of justice" (Renda 1983: 153). The combination of *omertà* (the code of silence) among the population and the complicity of high-ranking politicians and public functionaries insured the almost certain acquittal of those *mafiosi* who were brought to trial. In fact, a long record of acquittals for lack of sufficient evidence came to be one of the hallmarks of the "true" *mafioso*.

Despite the recurrent use or threat of violence which distinguishes the mafia from mere corruption, the mafia boss within his own community was considered not a criminal, but rather a community leader—prestigious, influential, and respected as well as feared. The career of the typical *mafioso* passed through two distinct stages. The first was the competition for honor and wealth in a Hobbesian universe without social or legal constraints and the affirmation, through the commission of acts of violence, of the mafioso as a "man of respect." The second stage could be considered one of "institutionalization." Domination through physical force was translated into authority, and the status of the *mafioso* rose from criminal to respected member of the local elite, recognized and legitimated by the representatives of legal power. This required the passage from self-affirmation through violence to the containment and management of conflict within the *mafioso*'s territorial domain, as well as the creation of networks of social and political relations to sustain his position; in this stage of his career the *mafioso* was seen by the authorities as a "man of order." The mafia thus served as an important channel of social mobility in an otherwise rigid class structure. The traditional mafia boss would be seen in the company of the mayor, the local parliamentary deputy or cabinet minister, the priest, and the carabinieri—he was on intimate terms with the entire local elite and at times even formally a part of it.

18

Emblematic of the traditional *mafioso* are the careers of Calogero Vizzini and Giuseppe Genco Russo, reputed to be the most powerful mafia bosses of the 1940s and 1950s. Vizzini, of peasant origin and semi-literate, became *gabelloto* of a large estate as well as a sulphur mine in central Sicily; as a representative of a consortium of sulphur mine operators, he even participated in high-level meetings in Rome and London concerning government subsidies and tariffs. When the Allies landed in Sicily, Vizzini's reputation was such that he was nominated mayor of his hometown, Villalba; in the postwar period, he initially supported the Separatist movement and subsequently joined the Christian Democratic Party. Upon Vizzini's death in 1954, his successor was Giuseppe Genco Russo. Like Vizzini, Genco Russo was of peasant origin and, through a career of violence stretching from the 1920s to the 1940s, established his position as a "man of honor;" during that period he was arrested repeatedly on charges ranging from theft and extortion to membership in a criminal association to murder and, with one exception, regularly acquitted on grounds of insufficient evidence (the mark of the successful *mafioso*). In 1944 the court granted Genco Russo a decree of rehabilitation for his one conviction, thereby allowing him "to recreate a moral and social virginity, acquiring a respectability which will permit him to undertake even political activity" (Antimafia Commission 1972, Vol. 1: 379). This political activity consisted initially in support for the Separatist and Monarchist causes (he was awarded the honorific title of Cavaliere della Corona d'Italia in 1946), and then for the Christian Democratic Party, of which he became a local leader and town councillor in the 1960s. Genco Russo's description of himself and of his role in the community provide an eloquent illustration of the self-image of the *mafioso* in the second, "legitimate" stage of his career—the *mafioso* as a public benefactor rather than as a dangerous criminal:

> It's in my nature. I have no ulterior motives. If I can do a man a favor, no matter who he is, I will; because that's how I'm made... .I can't say 'no' to anyone. The trouble I'm put to is not so great that I have to refuse people in need.... Very often warm-heartedness will win a man

19

gratitude and friendship, and then the time
comes to ask for one thing or another... .Folks
come and ask how they should vote because
they feel the need for advice. They want to
show that they are grateful to those who have
worked for their good; they want to thank them
for what they've done by voting for them; but
they are ignorant, and want to be told how to do
it (Dolci 121-122).

Vizzini and Genco Russo also illustrate another essential characteristic of the mafia—its capacity to adapt to changing economic,
social and political circumstances. Although the mafia often
employed violence to resist change, it also proved capable of
manipulating popular movements or progressive reforms for its
own ends. We have already seen evidence of such adaptability in
the mafia's reaction to the breakdown of feudalism, Italian unification, and the introduction of democratic institutions. During the
socialist movement of the Sicilian Fasci in the 1890s and the
peasant land occupations in the aftermaths of the First and
Second World Wars, the mafia responded with a dual strategy.
On the one hand, as shown above, the mafia served as an instrument of armed repression against leftist movements; on the other,
it took over the new organizational forms and turned them from
vehicles of class mobilization into means for perpetuating traditional social values and relationships. Both Vizzini and Genco
Russo organized peasant cooperatives during both postwar
periods, through which they deflected the appeal of the left-wing
parties, maintained their hold over the peasants, and guaranteed
their own continued access to the land. When land reform was
finally enacted in 1950, *mafiosi* were in a position to perform their
traditional role of brokerage between the peasants, the landlords,
and the state. They were able to exploit the intense land hunger
of the peasants, gain concessions from the landlords in return for
limiting the impact of the reform, and make substantial profits
from their mediation in land sales. Once again, one sees the
fusion of economic gain with functions of social and political
control.

Raimondo Catanzaro has argued that the essence of the mafia and the explanation for its persistence in the face of dramatic changes in economic, social, and political conditions lies in a process of "social hybridization:"

> mafia groups are not relics of the past, but were formed as a result of a specific combination of ancient and modern, a mixture of private violence and the legitimate violence of the state, of competition for economic resources in the market and the absence of regulatory standards for economic activities other than violence... . - [O]ne of the fundamental models of behaviour for the mafia consists in resistance to social changes but, when these changes appear inevitable, to exploit them for its own ends... . One of the consequences of this model of behaviour is that new institutions come to be utilized for the fulfillment of traditional values. A double process thus occurs: on one side, the modern institutions are modified and employed for ends other than those for which they were originally intended. On the other, the traditional values do not disappear; they are not replaced by new values, but are adapted to make traditional use of new institutions (Catanzaro 1985: 34, 45-46).[18]

Thus, far from falling victim to processes of modernization, as many observers of the traditional mafia predicted, *mafiosi* emerged instead as protagonists of change, as will become dramatically evident in an examination of the period from the mid-1950s on.

In conclusion, the traditional mafia should be seen as a system of violent clienteles, an integral part of a chain of patron-client relations linking the Sicilian peasant to the holders of national political power. In return for his vote and for other potentially less savory services the peasant received protection and a variety of small favors from the *mafioso*, who in turn received protection, legitimation, and access to public resources from more highly placed patrons among the dominant political and economic elites in return for the key social and political functions which he performed. Far from challenging the power or status of the dominant elite, the successful *mafioso* became part of that elite.

21

Far from substituting itself for the state or constituting an autonomous state within the state, as many analyses of the mafia have suggested, the traditional mafia functioned in a symbiotic relationship with the state, depending on the state insofar as a substantial part of its power was rooted either in the delegation of certain functions from the central government or in privileged access to critical levers of state power and patronage. It was precisely this relationship of *mafiosi* to the dominant classes and to public authorities which rendered them immune to any state-based action against them.[19]

The successful *mafioso* became an integral part of the power structure, a solid pillar of support for the forces opposing transformation of the existing social order. In the words of the Antimafia Commission of the Italian Parliament, a source which cannot be suspected of political bias, "One can conclude that the mafia was in its origins not a phenomenon of the subordinate classes, as such excluded from any power agreement, but, on the contrary, a phenomenon of those classes which at the moment of Unification already dominated (and continued to dominate) the political and economic life of the island—the feudal nobility and the great landowners" (Antimafia Commission 1976: 112).

The Fascist Interlude and the Re-emergence of the Mafia in the Postwar Period

With the Fascist takeover in 1922, the functions of social control and political mediation which were so crucial to the legitimation of the mafia in the eyes of dominant elites rapidly lost their raison d'être. Once the Fascist dictatorship was firmly established and elections abolished, many large landowners, recognizing in the Fascist state an equally effective and less burdensome means of maintaining public order and social stability, did not hesitate to sacrifice their former allies to the new regime: "Where the Fascist State guaranteed vested landed interests and established effective security in the countryside, *mafiosi* were rendered obsolete" (Blok 182). Nor, in the absence of elections, did they any longer hold any meaningful leverage over regional and national political leaders. The Fascist Prefect of Palermo, Cesare Mori, clearly understood the bases of mafia power when he argued that, in order to defeat the mafia, it was necessary to

> forge a direct bond between the population and the state, to annul the system of intermediation under which citizens could not approach the authorities except through middlemen..., receiving as a favor that which is due them as their right (cited in Catanzaro, 1988: 141).

Once its dominance was secured, Fascism tolerated no rival power structures. The Fascist Party took over the mafia's role of political intermediation, while the Fascist state firmly reasserted its monopoly over the use of violence, unleashing a fierce campaign of repression from 1925 to 1929 under the direction of Mori. Mori did not hesitate to use police state methods, suspending legal guarantees, ordering mass arrests of guilty and innocent alike, and mounting a veritable state of siege in some rural communities. However, despite claims that the mafia had been eliminated, only minor and middle-level *mafiosi* fell into Mori's net. The most influential mafia leaders had by this time become quite respectable; many were closely linked to noted politicians or influential members of Palermo society. When Mori in his enthusiasm became so imprudent as to denounce figures such as these, thereby threatening the very political class upon whose support Fascism depended, he was soon fired, and the much-hailed war on the mafia abruptly ceased.[20]

Thus, while the more obviously criminal elements of the mafia were arrested and exiled, the top-level mafia bosses assumed positions of power and prestige within the Fascist regime itself. Fascism succeeded in stamping out the mafia as a criminal organization by providing a more efficient substitute. It succeeded in monopolizing political power and the use of violence without, however, transforming the social and economic conditions in which the mafia had flourished. It was thus no surprise that the mafia re-emerged as soon as Fascism fell, elections were re-established, and the democratic state once again proved unable, without

23

recourse to private violence, to guarantee landed property against the onslaught of the peasant masses.

The re-emergence of the mafia is closely linked to the Allied invasion and occupation of Sicily in 1943. In planning the invasion, American intelligence services had established contacts with American mafia bosses and through them with their counterparts in Sicily in order to prepare the ground for the Allied forces. Upon landing in Sicily, the Allied Military Government—like the pre-Fascist Italian state—needed the support of local elites in order to govern. Because of their positions of local authority, their record of persecution under the Fascist regime, and their willingness to cooperate with the Allies, noted *mafiosi* were nominated to head local administrations in many of the communes of western Sicily.[21] They thus took up once again their traditional functions of political and economic brokerage, mediating between the population and an "alien" government, as well as taking advantage of the substantial sources of enrichment opened up by the wartime economy, especially in the black market. Some even held official positions in the Allied administration, like Vito Genovese (an American gangster who had returned to Italy during the Fascist period to avoid arrest), who was an aide and interpreter to Colonel Charles Poletti, the American military governor. This re-legitimation of the mafia as a privileged partner of the Allied occupation force and its placement in key positions of public power laid the foundation for the rapid penetration of the mafia into the politics and administration of Sicily in the postwar period.

In the months immediately following the Allied landing, the dominant political force in Sicily was the Separatist movement. Although the movement succeeded in arousing widespread popular support, its leadership remained firmly in the hands of the large landowners and their principal ally, the mafia. Behind the rhetoric of colonial oppression by the mainland, the real concern of the Separatist leaders (as seen in their support for the bandit Giuliano) was to defend their property against attack by the peasants and to protect themselves against the prospect of a Left-dominated government in Rome that might undermine their power and privileges. With the granting of Sicilian autonomy in 1946, the

24

Separatist movement collapsed, and the landowners and *mafiosi* shifted their support to the remnants of the pre-Fascist parties— the Liberals and Monarchists—in opposition to the forces of reform represented by the three mass parties—the Communists, Socialists, and Christian Democrats. The onset of the Cold War and the ejection of the left-wing parties from the national government in 1947, however, radically transformed the political climate and political alignments. As the standard bearer of democracy and Christianity against the Communist threat, the Christian Democratic Party (DC) found itself increasingly compelled to seek allies among the conservative forces on its right. As a result of the growing anti-Communism of the DC and of its overwhelming victory in the parliamentary elections of 1948 (conducted as a choice between East and West), the landowners and *mafiosi* came to see in the DC the expression of those same forces of social conservation in the name of which they had led the Separatist struggle. It would not be long before many of the most powerful mafia bosses of western Sicily, astutely perceiving where their best interests lay (the power of the mafia having always relied, as we have seen, upon a symbiotic relationship with the holders of political power), would deploy their impressive vote-gathering capabilities under the banner of Christian Democracy. Thus, while the DC continued to speak the language of a progressive mass party, its organizational structures in Sicily increasingly came to depend upon traditional channels of political influence, mediation, and control.[22]

The Great Transformation

From the mid-1950s on, the model of the traditional mafia (at least in its rural guise) experienced a deepening crisis as a result of processes of social, economic, and political change which transformed the face of the Italian South. The most important of these processes were mass emigration from the countryside, a vast increase in state intervention in the South, and, linked to the previous two, the explosive growth of the large coastal cities (especially marked in the cases of Palermo and Naples). Between 1950 and 1975 about 4 million people, primarily peasants and day

25

laborers, left southern Italy to seek industrial jobs in the North or in the countries of central and northern Europe. This massive exodus from the countryside led to the inexorable disintegration of traditional peasant society and, by providing peasants with an alternative short of long-term overseas migration, considerably weakened the leverage of the landowners and the mafia over local society. Even more important was the expansion of the Italian welfare state and the decision to use the power and resources of the state to carry out far-reaching programs of social and economic change in the South.

With the enactment of agrarian reform in 1950, twenty percent of agricultural land in Sicily and two-thirds of the land occupied by the *latifondo* passed from large estates to small holders (Renda 1985: 63). Yet, although its function as armed guardian of the great estates and privileged intermediary between the peasants and the landed elite came to an end, the mafia did not disappear with the disappearance of the *latifondo*. The mafia did not abandon the countryside, but rather turned its sights to new sources of power and gain, in particular the newly established programs of regional and national intervention, at that time oriented almost exclusively toward provision of rural infrastructures. As noted above, *mafiosi* imposed their intermediation in the land transactions resulting from the agrarian reform and were quick to take advantage of new policies for the modernization of agriculture, coming to dominate agricultural cooperatives (financed by contributions from the regional government), *consorzi di bonifica* (land reclamation and improvement agencies), and rural credit institutions, as well as claiming a disproportionate share of the agricultural subsidies and public works contracts given out by the Region and the Cassa per il Mezzogiorno (the newly established agency for the development of the South). All these sources of economic gain laid the basis for a process of financial accumulation which would subsequently assist the entry of the mafia into new and even more lucrative economic arenas.

Thus, processes of state-sponsored development did not lead to the destruction of the mafia but rather to its expansion and reinforcement in new fields of endeavor. Despite continued mafia interests in the countryside, by the mid-1950s it had become clear

26

to the rural elite, landowners and *mafiosi* alike, that the promise of economic gain now loomed largest in the coastal cities, whose tremendous population growth since the war had opened vast new possibilities for enrichment, from traditional sectors of mafia control like the wholesale produce, meat, and fish markets to the booming construction industry fueled by rapid urban expansion (all sectors, however, where public' regulation made political ties crucial for economic success). By the late 1950s, the mafia's grasp extended into virtually every sector of the economy of Palermo, still the economic and administrative capital of Sicily.

The extraordinary capability of the mafia to adapt to rapidly changing social, economic, and political conditions after World War II, once again belying any description of it as an archaic phenomenon, a vestige of traditional society, was to a large extent made possible by its political connections. In its increasing concentration on the urban arena, the mafia's links to political power, and in particular to the Christian Democratic Party, were further reinforced. In the words of the 1972 majority report of the parliamentary Antimafia Commission:

> The most conspicuous causal factor behind the persistence and expansion of mafia power in Sicily is undoubtedly the relationships which the mafia was able to establish with the public sector, above all with administrative and bureaucratic structures and then with political power (Antimafia Commission 1972, Vol. 1: 114).

The nature of the linkages between the DC and this new urban mafia is most evident in the sector of real-estate speculation and construction, both because of the magnitude of the interests at stake and because of the direct responsibility of local administrations, dominated by the Christian Democrats, for regulation of these activities. Control over the tempestuous processes of urban development which swept Italy in the postwar period has constituted the most important instrument of local political power, especially in the South where such power was exercised primarily along personalistic lines. Mafia penetration of this key sector of the urban economy took place at several levels: (1) preferential

27

access to credit, both from commercial banks and from regional credit institutions; (2) the winning of lucrative public contracts, from the public works projects of the Region to services like street maintenance contracted out by the city; (3) the complicity of the municipal administration in repeated abuses regarding the elaboration and implementation of the city plan, the awarding of building permits, and surveillance over construction projects; (4) a tight system of control over the construction sites themselves, with the mafia serving as an obligatory intermediary in the provision of building supplies and labor, as well as imposing its traditional "protection" system, with the price of refusal at best an exemplary theft and at worst a charge of dynamite. By the early 1970s the construction industry in the city of Palermo was almost entirely controlled by the mafia. The 1972 and 1976 reports of the Antimafia Commission underlined the political roots of such a situation, arguing that "there exists a parallel between the particular intensity of the criminal phenomenon and the administrative situation of a city of the importance of Palermo," which had, in the 1960s, "reached unprecedented heights in the unprincipled non-observance of the law, leaving behind irregularities of every kind" (Antimafia Commission 1972, Vol. 1: 877; Antimafia Commission 1976: 217).[23]

The changes in the social and economic milieu in which the mafia operated were reflected in a change in the political climate as well. In the early 1960s, a bloody war between rival *cosche* broke out in Palermo for control of the increasingly profitable economic opportunities brought about by rapid urban growth. The ferocity of the struggle was unprecedented, reaping 68 victims from 1961 to 1963 and culminating in the "massacre of Ciaculli" on June 30, 1963, when an automobile loaded with explosives and left outside the home of one of the warring bosses, exploded and killed seven police and military officers sent to defuse it. The tremendous public reaction to this event was a determining factor in provoking the immediate convocation of the special parliamentary commission to investigate the causes of the re-emergence of mafia violence in Sicily (known as the Antimafia Commission), which had been established six months earlier but never convened because of conflicting political pressures. The creation of the

28

Antimafia Commission marked a turning point in the traditional relationship between the mafia and the Italian state. The central government affirmed its intent to reappropriate its monopoly over the use of physical violence, withdrew the tacit delegation to the mafia of substantial powers for the maintenance of public order, and, for the first time since the 1920s, launched a serious campaign of repression against the mafia. These measures showed results in a sharp decline in mafia violence after 1963, such that many observers began to speak of the final stage of the struggle against the mafia, which was seen as having lost many of its traditional characteristics and subcultural ties and degenerated into urban "gangsterism"—more isolated and therefore more easily extirpated.

The mafia warfare of the 1960s did in fact signal the emergence of a new generation of *mafiosi*. The withdrawal of the delegation of functions of social control by the state and the passage of functions of economic and political intermediation in large part from the mafia to the mass political parties, in particular the DC, undermined the sources of legitimation which had in the past led *mafiosi* to be recognized as respected members of the local elite. As a result, the communitarian base of their power began to erode, giving way to a more exclusive reliance on the pursuit of economic gain through violence. Although traditional *mafiosi* like Vizzini and Genco Russo had utilized violence to establish their position in the first phase of their careers, in the second stage they limited recourse to violence, turned to primarily legal sources of gain, and exercised their power in an open and legitimate fashion. The new generation, on the other hand, does not share that dimension of openly acknowledged community power. Their activities remain to a large extent in the illegal sector (in particular the drug trade), and their adult lives are passed, not in the public exercise of a position of respect and influence, but in prison or in hiding from the authorities. The nature of their economic activities inspires intense competition, such that recourse to violence—increasingly brutal and often indiscriminate—cannot be abandoned for more legitimate pursuits. In the eyes of the public, respect has to a large extent been replaced by fear.

Despite this transformation, the mafia was not so easily defeated. Under the mask of quiescence it reorganized, regained lost ground, and expanded into new activities. The continued existence and political clout of the mafia are evidenced by the fate of the Antimafia Commission itself. Although the Commission collected volumes of evidence and produced reports unequivocal in their portrayal of political collusion, no action—either judicial or legislative—was taken in response to its revelations or recommendations until a decade later, by which time, as we shall see, the mafia had reconsolidated its position on quite new and even more powerful grounds.

Behind the headlines, however, the real protagonists of the period from the mid-1950s to the mid-1970s in western Sicily were not the *mafiosi*, but a new generation of political elites, who had succeeded in transforming the Christian Democratic Party, by now solidly entrenched in power at both the national and regional levels, from a loose coalition of traditional notables into a powerful political machine controlling all major centers of political, administrative, and economic power at the local level.[24] While the national DC was deeply divided by factional struggle, in western Sicily one faction, the *fanfaniani* (the followers of the national leader, Amintore Fanfani), had succeeded by the early 1960s in gaining a monopoly hold over all levers of local power. Because of the tremendous expansion of state economic and social intervention in the South and the progressive interpenetration of the DC and the state administration through the party's permanent hold on national power, the Christian Democrats became above all a party of mass patronage, the managers of a vast network of *clientela* relations reaching into every sector of southern society. As the scope of state intervention increased and the state administration became increasingly a fiefdom of the governing parties, the lines between the state and civil society blurred. In the words of Sidney Tarrow, there was a "privatization of state power for personal political aims" (Tarrow 327), as the state was transformed into a reservoir of patronage resources with which to build political careers and party fortunes. This new class of political brokers directly controlled the flow of public resources through the mass party and its privileged access to the centers of

state power, thereby taking over the key function of intermediation previously performed by *mafiosi*.

The creation of a highly centralized patronage-based machine in
Sicily was not due only to the privileged access of local DC
leaders to the levers of national power. Equally important was
the existence of an autonomous regional government, created in
1946 to forestall the Separatist threat. Unlike the majority of the
Italian regions, which only gained limited autonomy in 1970, the
Sicilian Region was granted substantial independent power and
resources, in particular in the spheres of social and economic
policy. With its massive budget and elephantine bureaucracy
(both in the regional offices themselves and in a series of special
economic agencies dealing with every aspect of the Sicilian
economy), the Region has become the heart of a vast patronage
machine. Like the national government, the Sicilian Region has
been controlled by the Christian Democratic Party since its
inception. The staffing of the regional bureaucracy, until 1963
carried out almost entirely on a patronage basis rather than
through competitive examinations, provided the occasion for the
direct integration of political clienteles (including *mafiosi*) into
public positions with strategic importance for the political and
economic life of Sicily.[25] The penetration of the mafia into the
regional government was criticized in the following terms by the
parliamentary Antimafia Commission:

> Instead of presenting itself as the antithesis of
> mafia methods and mentality, the Region created
> new and conspicuous opportunities for the
> practice of illegality, protectionism, and intrigue—
> that is, all that ordinarily constitutes the ideal
> *humus* for the mafia (Antimafia 1976: 1202-3).

Because of the effective centralization of power in Sicily in the
hands of a cohesive political elite with strong ties to national
power, it has been argued that the mafia, although it continued to
provide votes in return for complicity and protection, was rele-
gated to a subordinate role in the *clientela* pyramid (Arlacchi
1986: 69-71). Given the tremendous growth of state intervention
in the South and the resulting expansion of the patronage resour-

ces of the national and regional governments, political elites, while often not refusing the aid proffered by *mafiosi*, had developed independent economic and political resources and therefore were not as reliant on these local influence brokers as politicians had been in the past. The control over key resources was reversed. Now it was the political elites who controlled the public works contracts, building permits, and access to credit that the *mafiosi* needed for the successful pursuit of their new economic endeavors. However, the mass of evidence collected by the Antimafia Commission points less to control of the mafia by the politicians than to what has been termed an "organic interpenetration" between the interests of political elites and those of mafia bosses (Chinnici and Santino 130-134). According to the 1972 report of the Antimafia Commission,

> In this period the mafia no longer represented, as it had before, the defense of certain class interests or positions. It sought, as always, stable and concrete ties with bureaucratic structures and political circles, but it sought them for the direct advantages which they could provide in the exercise of the mafia's own illicit activities... . The individuals compromised with the mafia found the counterpart to their support not only in the usual electoral and political advantages, but also in a concrete co-participation in certain business affairs and speculative deals (Antimafia Commission 1972, Vol. 1: 147).

In such a situation it is difficult to say who manipulated whom. Whereas previously, despite their close relationship, the roles of the *mafioso* and the politician had for the most part remained distinct, they were now tightly intertwined in the pursuit of economic gain. Thus, by the 1970s the situation could best be characterized not as political control of the mafia but rather as government *with* the mafia—a concrete and intimate partnership in the pursuit of wealth and power.

From the Entrepreneurial to the Financial Mafia

The mafia of the 1980s presents a quite different face from the traditional agrarian mafia of the 1950s or even the urban mafia of the 1960s. The most drastic difference lies in the level and the targets of mafia violence. Until the late 1970s mafia violence was directed primarily against other *mafiosi* (in periodic struggles for dominance), against individuals who refused to submit to mafia ultimatums, or, when such violence became political, against the leaders of opposition parties or popular movements which challenged mafia power. Members of the dominant elite or official representatives of the state were rarely threatened by the mafia. On the contrary, as we have seen, they tended, either directly or indirectly, to be the allies rather than the enemies of the mafia. In the 1980s, however, the mafia seems to have launched an all-out attack on the Italian state. From 1979 through 1988, three magistrates, five high-ranking police officials, one journalist, four politicians (the regional secretary of the Communist Party, the provincial secretary of the Christian Democratic Party, a former Christian Democratic mayor of Palermo, and the Christian Democratic President of the Sicilian Region), and most shocking of all, General Carlo Alberto Dalla Chiesa, the so-called "super-prefect" sent to Palermo to head the struggle against the mafia, were assassinated in Palermo. How can this radical transformation in the relationship between the mafia and the Italian state be explained?

In the only comprehensive study yet to appear on the changes which have taken place in the mafia in the 1970s and 1980s, Pino Arlacchi points to the emergence of a new entrepreneurial mafia which not only has assumed an important and growing role in the economy (both legal and illegal) of large areas of southern Italy, but also has extended its hold into geographic areas and economic sectors outside its traditional spheres of influence (Arlacchi, 1986). The mafia of the 1980s is no longer a regional phenomenon, confined to Sicily or southern Italy, but instead an economic and financial power of national and international dimensions.

In using the term "entrepreneurial mafia," Arlacchi argues that a profound transformation has taken place from a "pre-modern" mafia whose economic base consisted primarily of "parasitical" activities (extortion, tribute money, and the like) to a dynamic

33

"capitalist" mafia investing its illicit gains in productive activities forming an integral part of a modern economy. As social and economic conditions have evolved, the mafia has transformed its role from one of mediation ("rent capitalism" or "broker capitalism") to a more directly entrepreneurial role, not abandoning illicit activities but using them to finance processes of capital accumulation and reinvestment in the legal sector. However, the distinction between a traditional and a modern mafia is perhaps less clear-cut. Although Arlacchi dates this transformation from the 1970s, the evidence presented in the earlier sections of this monograph suggests that, in the Sicilian case at least, the mafia has from the outset operated in both illegal and legal markets and combined "parasitical" with "entrepreneurial" activities (e.g., its role in the construction industry in a city like Palermo from the mid-1950s on).

Arlacchi provides a fascinating description of the advantages which the *mafioso* as entrepreneur enjoys over his competitors (Arlacchi 1986: 109-125). These advantages are directly linked to Catanzaro's concept of "social hybridization"—the fusion of tradition and innovation which is central to explaining the persistence of the mafia and its continuing economic success in the face of tremendous social, economic and political changes. The *mafioso* has effectively adapted traditional values and methods to the pursuit of profit in a modern capitalist economy. His first competitive advantage lies in his ability to discourage competition. Through the threat or exercise of violence, *mafiosi* have not only discouraged private investment in large areas of the South, but have succeeded in establishing virtual territorial monopolies of certain economic activities—e.g., the cycle of construction-related activities in the city of Palermo, tourist-related construction on large tracts of the southern Italian coast, and, perhaps most striking, control of seventy percent of the sub-contracts for the construction of a publicly financed industrial port at Gioia Tauro in Calabria in the mid-1970s.[26]

A second advantage lies in the *mafioso*'s ability to secure his labor force at lower cost and with fewer restrictions than can his competitors. Here the advantages lie in non-payment of social security and other benefits, as well as in the recruitment of a more docile and flexible labor force than would otherwise be the case.

34

A combination of personal ties and potential repression discourages worker organization and conflictuality and increases productivity. In this regard, the *mafioso* can often exploit traditional family, territorial, and subcultural ties while conducting business deals with national or even international ramifications.

Finally, the *mafioso* has at his disposal financial resources far superior to those of the normal firm. In contrast to the businessman who must rely on outside financing through bank loans, paying high interest rates and suffering lengthy bureaucratic delays, the *mafioso* has two critical advantages—privileged access to credit through his political and financial connections and a substantial reserve of liquidity based on the profits from his illegal activities. Unlike most other firms, the mafioso often faces the problem of *excess* liquidity, leading him to seek ever new investment possibilities.

The expansion of the scope and scale of the mafia's entrepreneurial activities is not sufficient, however, to explain the emergence of the mafia as a profound challenge to the power and legitimacy of the democratic state in the 1980s. On the one hand, the expanding power of the mafia is linked to the deterioration of economic, social, and political conditions in much of the South throughout the 1980s. As has been demonstrated above, the penetration of the post-war Italian state into the South—in terms of both economic development policies and the extension of social welfare programs—created a fertile terrain for renewed mafia infiltration of public administration and mafia access to the substantial flows of public funds which resulted from those policies. By the late 1970s it had become clear that these policies had not created a process of self-sustaining economic development in the South, but rather an "assisted economy," increasingly dependent upon public resources to sustain consumption and consensus. Under the impact of the economic crisis, state spending in the South declined, the limited industrial initiatives created in the preceding decade faltered, and levels of unemployment rose sharply.[27] The social and economic fabric of the South became increasingly fragile, social deviance increased sharply, and competition for scarce resources became more and more intense. The large cities harbored a growing marginal proletariat, excluded from stable employment. Competition for increasingly scarce resources from the center provoked severe factional struggle within the Christian Democratic Party and between the DC and its coalition partners, paralyzing many local and regional administrations and thereby reducing the capacity of the new class of political brokers to manage tensions through the politics of mass patronage, which they had so adeptly perfected in the preceding decade. The interlocking system of political, social, and economic power constructed by the DC in the 1950s and 1960s began to erode, opening new spaces for other forces.

Even more importantly, a major transformation in the nature and scope of the mafia's economic activities, in both the illegal and the legal spheres, occurred as a result of the movement of the Sicilian mafia in the mid-1970s into a leading position in the international drug trade. The liquidity which made the movement of the mafia into the sector of heroin refinement (as opposed to the lesser intermediary role which it had previously undertaken) was based upon the surplus profits from the activities of the two preceding decades. In addition to the profits from traditional illicit activities (extortion, kidnapping, traffic in contraband cigarettes), it is striking that a substantial portion of the capital available for investment in the drug trade can be traced directly to mafia penetration of the public administration. One such source of investment capital was profits from the construction industry, made possible, as we have seen, by collusion with local administrators. A second source was the agricultural subsidies' disbursed by the Sicilian Region, a disproportionate share of which ended up in the hands of *mafiosi*.[28]

A third source was the enormous profits reaped from tax collections which, from 1952 until 1982, were subcontracted by the regional government to private collection agencies at rates of 10% in contrast to a national average of 3.3%. The dangers inherent in the tremendous liquidity accumulated by the private tax collectors (*esattori*) in Sicily and the suspected ties to the mafia of the most powerful of the *esattori*, the Salvos, one of the island's wealthiest families and prominent supporters of the DC, were denounced already in the 1976 report of the Antimafia Commission (although to no effect) and are outlined in still greater detail in the documents prepared by the magistrates for the "maxi-trial" against 707 *mafiosi* held in Palermo between February 1986 and December

1987 (Antimafia Commission 1976: 601-603; Stajano 313-358).
Finally, and most importantly, one must look more closely at the relationship of the mafia to the banking system. Not only, as noted above, has privileged access to the banking system provided *mafiosi* with a competitive advantage over legitimate entrepreneurs. It has also been crucial for the recycling of illicit gains (especially from the drug trade) into national and international financial circuits and into "clean" investments. The linkages between the mafia and the banking system take three forms. First, through their political allies *mafiosi* have had privileged access to major credit institutions in Sicily, the boards of directors of which are subject to political appointment. Second, the mafia has penetrated and often directly controls a vast and growing network of small rural banks in Sicily, the numbers of which have multiplied far out of proportion to economic growth. For example, in the period from 1952 to 1984 the entire network of minor banks in Sicily expanded by 270.9% as compared to an increase of only 76.9% in all of Italy; even more telling, the *banchi popolari*, the specific form of local bank which has been most under investigation by the magistrates, increased by 681.1% in contrast to a figure of 108.5% for all of Italy.[29] As a result, Sicily, which produces 5.6% of Italy's GDP, accounts for 8.8% of the country's bank branches (Cusimano 111). This expansion of the banking system in Sicily is in turn directly linked to politics. As part of the special provisions of Sicilian autonomy granted in 1946, the Sicilian regional government exercises powers over financial institutions (in particular the authorization for the opening of new banking outlets) that in the rest of Italy are reserved to the Minister of the Treasury or the Bank of Italy. Given the evidence presented above with regard to mafia penetration of the political parties and the institutions of local government in Sicily, one should not be surprised at the growing evidence of mafia influence over the very shape of the banking system as well.

While the direct production of heroin in Sicily was rendered possible by the excess liquidity accumulated through the sources outlined above, it represented in turn a qualitative leap from earlier mafia activities—an extension of the "entrepreneurial" mafia into what one might term the "financial" mafia. Given the magnitude and complexity of the drug traffic, there was a move toward a more centralized organizational structure, a kind of informal hierarchy or "Commission" composed of the heads of the most important families and reflecting the internal equilibrium among the various groups at any given time. As was stressed at the outset, however, this should not be seen as a rigid or monolithic chain of command, a kind of corporate bureaucracy, but rather as the expression of temporary alliances among powerful contenders who still retain important sources of autonomy. Although the vastly increased scope of its economic activities has led the mafia and the constellation of economic and financial interests which have formed around it to appear increasingly as an impersonal market force, a kind of multinational corporation of crime, the success of mafia "enterprises" continues to rely in the last analysis on the personal "charisma" of the *capo-mafia* and on networks of personal trust rather than legal-contractual guarantees. This personal basis of mafia power impedes its transformation in a rational-bureaucratic sense toward more stable forms of organization and explains the continuing recourse to violence as an instrument of competition.

The magnitude of the economic interests at stake in the drug trade also required a vaster and more complex set of linkages to legal sectors of the economy and the financial system. In the first place, the mafia needed more solid and far-reaching financial connections than its local financial base could provide. Thus, it worked to penetrate into national and international financial circuits, an entry in which financiers like Michele Sindona and Roberto Calvi played a major role,[30] in order to acquire both financial capital and the financial linkages necessary for recycling the enormous profits (estimated at 700-800 billion lire per year— approximately 400-500 million dollars [Arlacchi 1986: 207]) from the drug trade. Secondly, *mafiosi* created, or further expanded a network of legal enterprises—especially in the areas of construction, public works, tourism, and agriculture—to serve as channels for the reinvestment of illegal gains.[31] The scope of its economic transactions has transformed the mafia into an economic and financial power of national and international dimensions, a kind of multinational holding company.

This tremendous expansion in the economic base of the mafia (in both quantitative and territorial terms) has had several important consequences. Both its illegitimate and legitimate economic activities have contributed to a renewed social consensus in support of the mafia. To a large extent this consensus has been based on the mafia's capacity to provide concrete solutions to basic needs not answered by public institutions. For example, the mafia has responded to a serious housing shortage in urban areas in the South by constructing millions of illegal units (obviously taking advantage of either the complicity or the impotence of local administrators). And through its own economic activities and continued access to channels of public spending (for example, the mafia and the *camorra* succeeded in appropriating a substantial chunk of the funds for reconstruction after the earthquakes of 1968 in Sicily and 1980 in Campania), the mafia creates jobs and wealth—a kind of mafia "welfare state" in juxtaposition to the faltering official welfare state undercut by economic crisis and by spiralling government deficits. Given the deterioration of the southern economy over the past decade, the increase in unemployment, especially among youth, and the deepening social and economic crisis of cities like Palermo and Naples, the mafia, the Calabrese 'ndrangheta, and the Neapolitan *camorra* have assumed growing importance both as legitimate employers and as recruiters of unemployed youth into the ranks of organized crime. Increasing sectors of the economy, especially but not only in the South, have become directly or indirectly dependent upon investment and employment produced by the mafia, both in the illicit activities linked to the drug trade or other mafia rackets and in the legitimate activities born of the recycling of illicit gains.[32] The area of consensus created by such employment extends even into sectors of the middle and professional classes, not themselves necessarily *mafiosi*, but performing important technical and managerial functions for mafia firms, as well as to legitimate entrepreneurs who, if they do not wish to be forced out, have little choice but to come to terms with the mafia.

The actual economic impact of the mafia in the South is the object of an ongoing debate among Italian scholars. Some, like Arlacchi, have argued that there has been a massive influx of investment of profits from illegal activities into legitimate business ventures, such that the mafia is now in a position to shape large sectors of the southern economy (Arlacchi, 1986). Others argue

Table 1. Labor Force Participation (as % of total population), 1971-1981

	1971	1981
Palermo (province)	36.80	26.62
Sicily	38.13	27.33
Calabria	42.38	28.93
Campania	41.05	27.61

instead that most mafia firms in the South remain small and traditional, with a high rate of turnover, and that they serve less as serious entrepreneurial efforts than as "fronts" for the recycling of illicit gains (Catanzaro, 1986a). These conflicting views raise broader questions as to the nature of the "mafia economy." (1) To what extent has the mafia reinvested in the South rather than channeling its funds into investments elsewhere in the country or into national and international financial circuits? (2) To the extent that the mafia has invested in the South, how much mafia generation of investment and employment has been in the legal rather than in the illegal sector? (3) Is the mafia a stimulus or an obstacle to further economic development in the South? Is the mafia taking on the role of the entrepreneurial bourgeoisie in the South (the weakness of which has historically constituted a serious impediment to autonomous development), or is it precisely the mafia which has prevented the emergence of indigenous entrepreneurship?

Any attempt to answer these questions on the basis of available statistical data is undermined by the absence of any reliable data on the illegal economy and by the often contradictory nature of existing data on the legal economy. Despite these caveats, a comparison of the 1971 and 1981 censuses for the regions where the presence of organized crime is strongest—Sicily, Calabria, and Campania—demonstrates certain trends. First, in each of the three regions, there has been a sharp decline in labor force participation[33] and a rapid increase in officially registered unemployment (see Table 1 and note 27). Second, each of the three regions has seen a decline in its index of industrialization between 1970 and 1984 (see note 27). Third, in each region there has been a decline in the percentage of the labor force engaged in industry (including construction), while substantial increases have occurred in

Table 2. Distribution of the Labor Force by Economic Sectors (in %),
1971/1981

	Industry*	Construction	Commerce	Services
Palermo (province)	20.50/16.20	13.44/12.99	12.69/17.35	21.56/30.39
Sicily	18.80/14.93	14.77/13.74	11.51/16.43	17.85/26.86
Calabria	15.30/10.74	21.03/17.11	8.71/12.92	15.52/26.68
Campania	24.90/21.31	13.14/ 9.65	11.50/14.56	19.11/24.42

*All industrial sectors except construction.

commerce and services (see Table 2). At the same time, there has been a sharp decrease in the number of industrial firms across the three regions, but huge increases in the number of construction firms and more contained increases in commerce (because of differences in the way the data were collected in 1971 and 1981, it was not possible to draw accurate comparisons in the service sector). However, the number of employees per firm remained quite low and actually decreased in the construction sector (see Table 3).

Table 3. Changes in number of firms, number of employees, and
employees per firm by economic sector, 1971/1981

	Industry*	Construction	Commerce
Palermo (province)			
No. of firms	-26.4%	+250.2%	+32.7%
No. of employees	+8.5%	+67.6%	+36.8%
Employees per firm	3.9/5.8	13.8/6.6	2.2/2.2
Sicily			
No. of firms	-33.0%	+154.3%	+33.4%
No. of employees	-7.6%	+30.0%	+38.7%
Employees per firm	3.4/4.7	9.8/4.9	1.9/2.0
Calabria			
No. of firms	-38.5%	+106.1%	+30.1%
No. of employees	-2.3%	+31.9%	+41.7%
Employees per firm	2.6/4.1	8.7/5.6	1.6/1.8
Campania			
No. of firms	-22.1%	+109.6%	+25.3%
No.of employees	+12.5%	+44.3%	+29.7%
Employees per firm	6.1/8.8	8.7/6.0	1.9/2.0

*All industrial sectors except construction.

What conclusions can be drawn from these trends? There is evidence of substantial increases in the numbers of legally registered firms in construction and commerce, and the probability is that there are still larger numbers of such firms unrecorded by the census, since these are sectors which in Italy are notorious for containing large numbers of "underground" enterprises, which fail to officially register in order to avoid regulation and payment of social-security contributions and the like. On the other hand, these sectors remain the reserve of tiny, often family-based firms, and appear, especially in construction, to have undergone still further fragmentation. This impression is reinforced by the data indicating declines in overall industrial employment (including construction) and increases only in commerce and services. Given the structure of the southern economy, where an already swollen tertiary sector has served primarily as a safety valve to absorb unemployment from other sectors in the absence of sustained industrial development, further expansion in the areas of commerce and services can hardly be taken as evidence of a substantial contribution of mafia investment to promoting the process of economic development in the South.

The limitations of available statistical data make the above conclusions extremely tentative. All analyses of the contemporary mafia agree that the mafia is playing an increasingly important economic role in the South. It is also clear from judicial investigations that substantial flows of funds from the illegal to the legal sector have occurred. What remains unclear from available data is the nature of such investment. The evidence presented above seems to suggest either that mafia investment may be to a large extent rechanneled back into illicit activities in the South (which could indeed provide substantial employment, but which would not show up in official statistics), with legal firms serving primarily as "fronts," or that the mafia is directing a major portion of its gains into investment channels outside the South.

Regardless of its origins (legal or illegal), the growing economic power and concomitant social consensus generated by the mafia in turn translate into growing political clout. Some observers have argued that in the 1980s the mafia assumed increasing autonomy vis-à-vis its traditional political allies, thereby explaining the unprecedented outburst of violence against representatives of the state and of the governing parties (Arlacchi 1986: 165-180). Two phenomena have been cited as evidence for this increasing political autonomy of the mafia. The first is the formation of "political-mafioso lobbies." These are joint ventures, based on shared economic interests, among mafia bosses, politicians, and represen-tatives of local and national entrepreneurial and financial elites for the purpose of influencing key centers of public power.[34] What is new is not so much the existence of such linkages, which have always characterized the Sicilian mafia and which were amply documented in the 1972 and 1976 reports of the Antimafia Com-mission, but rather the *level* of the political and financial connec-tions in question, which now extend far beyond the regional arena to touch the highest levels of the national political and financial systems and which have come to constitute a major force of corruption in Italian public life. One of the distinctive charac-teristics of the Italian case is precisely this facility of linkage both among different sectors of criminal elites and between such criminal elites and important sectors of official political and economic institutions, such that the line between legality and illegality has become increasingly ambiguous. Beginning in the early 1980s, a growing body of evidence has emerged not only with regard to the ties between mafia/*camorra* and their political/finan-cial allies, but pointing as well to connections with the P2 of Licio Gelli, right-wing terrorism, and the Italian secret services.[35]

The second indicator of the increasing political autonomy of the mafia is that *mafiosi*, or members of their families, have directly assumed elective and administrative positions, rather than dele-gating such functions to political intermediaries. This has been especially true at the local and regional levels. Given the paucity of autonomous economic resources in the South, local govern-ments—because of their role in land-use regulation and the dis-tribution of public funds in the form of contracts, subsidies, welfare payments, etc.—are crucial levers of economic power and of the organization of consensus, and as such have been key targets of mafia penetration. Here again the line between the criminal activities of the mafia and legal clientelism has become increasing-ly blurred. However, as the Sicilian experience demonstrates, the phenomenon itself is not new. What has gained attention is rather the increasing scope of such direct mafia/*camorra* political repre-

43

sentation, especially in Campania and Calabria, where the distinction between the political and criminal spheres seems until recently to have been more clear-cut.

The key to understanding the emergence of the mafia as a direct political protagonist in the 1980s lies in the relationship between economic resources and political power. The traditional autonomy of the mafia, based on control of a key resource—the land—and on the delegation by the Italian state of functions of social and political control in peripheral areas, came to an end in the 1950s. At this point, as shown above, the functions of intermediation and social control performed by the traditional mafia were assumed instead by a new class of political brokers, represented *par excellence* by the DC, which, through its control of the state and of the vast new programs of public spending in the South in the postwar period, monopolized the channels of access to key economic resources. As a result, the mafia, attracted by the outpouring of public resources in various forms, became increasingly enmeshed in the *clientela* networks controlled by DC notables and their political allies.

What transformed this relationship in the late 1970s was the dramatic change in the economic base of the mafia, engendered by the enormous profits from the drug trade. As its economic power grew to unprecedented proportions and spread from peripheral regions like Sicily to the national and international levels, the balance of power between the mafia and its traditional political allies began to shift. The mafia demanded an expansion in the scope of its political power commensurate with the explosion of its economic power, and thereby provoked a split in the ranks of those whose complicity or silence had traditionally protected it. At the same time, competition for control of the enormous economic interests at stake shattered the confederal organizational structure created to restrain conflict and led to a violent struggle for supremacy among rival *cosche*, leaving 606 dead in the province of Palermo alone between 1978 and 1984 (Chinnici and Santino 84).[36] Despite the impressive network of corruption and complicity which the mafia had constructed over the years, the government and the political parties could no longer look the other way when confronted with a massacre of these proportions. The mafia thus found itself increasingly up against magistrates, police officers, and

44

politicians whose actions could no longer be controlled or neutralized as in the past—and this precisely at a time when, given the dimensions of the economic interests at stake, the non-action of the police and the magistracy was critical. It was at this point that the mafia began to strike back with its weapons of last resort—intimidation and violence—this time directed against representatives of the state and the political parties.

It is thus the expanding economic power and the increasing political demands of the mafia which explain the violent conflict between the mafia and the Italian state—or, more accurately, certain sectors of the Italian state. Probably the most striking characteristic of the mafia of the 1980s is this shift from the "stabilizing" violence of the traditional mafia to the "destabilizing" violence of the present—what many observers have labelled "mafia terrorism." It should not be forgotten, however, that, in contrast to terrorism, the mafia has from its origins been an expression of the dominant classes. What one sees today is less a mafia which has rendered itself autonomous from the political system—to which, given the nature of many of its economic activities, close linkages and privileged access remain critical—than a struggle for hegemony among competing groups *within* the Italian state. In the words of one observer, "the dominant classes are seeing an old subordinate ally transformed into a dangerous competitor, armed with violence and great amounts of capital" (Santino 18). The mafia's traditional quest for legitimacy and respectability has come into conflict with the demands of capital accumulation. The latter have prevailed. Thus the turn to violence directed against representatives of the state is not an attempt to subvert or destroy the state, as in the case of the Red Brigades. Instead, it is an attempt to assure control of the state for the mafia and its political allies, and thereby to insure the continuation or restoration of a political status quo which guarantees the unfettered pursuit of mafia interests.

The Struggle Against the Mafia

Given the profound transformation in the nature and the economic base of the mafia, its increasingly national and international dimensions, and the growing violence of its attack on democratic institutions, what can be done to combat it? The assassination in September 1982 of General Carlo Alberto Dalla Chiesa, the "super-prefect" sent to Palermo to coordinate the battle against the mafia, marked an important turning point. Never before had the mafia struck so high. The audacity and brutality of the crime profoundly shook public opinion and political/governmental circles, until then lackluster in if not indifferent to the struggle against the mafia. In the wake of Dalla Chiesa's death, a series of tough new repressive measures were enacted. First, a new position was created, the High Commissioner for the struggle against the mafia, to replace Dalla Chiesa, and his successor was granted special powers even more far-reaching than those which had been obstinately refused the General when he was alive.[37] Secondly, Parliament enacted new legislation, the so-called Legge Rognoni-La Torre, providing magistrates for the first time with access to the banking system in order to carry out investigations of the bank accounts, economic activities, and investments of suspected *mafiosi*, and the power to confiscate property acquired through illicit means.[38] Although such measures had been proposed in 1976 by the Antimafia Commission and the legislation itself was introduced in 1980, it required the assassination of Dalla Chiesa to mobilize Parliament.

In the three regions most affected—Sicily, Campania, and Calabria—the Legge Rognoni-La Torre has provoked resistance among entrepreneurs and politicians on the grounds that the controls which it prescribes will strangle the local economy, thereby further increasing already high levels of unemployment and reducing public support for the anti-mafia struggle.[39] Due to the lack of an unequivocal political will and the absence of a coordinated plan of action, there have been great disparities among regions and among different sectors of the police forces in the zeal with which this legislation has been applied.[40] At the same time, despite political resistance and limited application, this legislation has played a central role in obtaining evidence to indict high-ranking mafia bosses and their political and entrepreneurial allies, heretofore

46

considered untouchable.

Armed with these investigatory powers, a small group of committed magistrates (the so-called *pretori d'assalto*) successfully reconstructed the activities of the "new mafia" of the 1970s and 1980s, on the basis of which unprecedented judicial proceedings ("maxi-trials") were initiated against hundreds of defendants in Palermo and Naples at the beginning of 1986.[41] The Palermo trial culminated in December 1987 with the conviction of 342 out of 456 defendants (among them several top-level mafia bosses sentenced to life imprisonment). Although these convictions are far from constituting a fatal blow to the Sicilian mafia, whose organization, according to many observers, remains largely intact, the trials represented a crucial landmark. As symbols of a highly visible and large-scale public commitment to the struggle against organized crime, they represented a first step in undermining the myth of invincibility which has for so long surrounded the mafia and thereby eroding a cultural climate which has tended, at least tacitly, to condone such activities.[42]

It is illusory, however, to believe that the mafia can be defeated through judicial measures alone. Just as the sources of its power are ultimately social, economic, and political, so must any solution go beyond purely repressive measures to strike at the social, economic, and political roots of such power. As demonstrated in the first part of this monograph, the mafia has traditionally enjoyed a certain social legitimacy, reinforced in recent years by its growing importance in the local economy. However, especially in the aftermath of the death of General Dalla Chiesa, important shifts in public opinion have taken place. These shifts are particularly marked in the case of the Church in the regions in question, which has for the first time made authoritative pronouncements denouncing the mafia,[43] and of the public school system, which has begun to stimulate discussion of the mafia in the classroom. While not sufficient in and of themselves, such initiatives are critical in order to isolate the mafia from the broader social-cultural context which has traditionally sustained it and to provide a broader base of public support for those individuals and groups within the political parties and the public administration who wish to undertake a serious struggle against the mafia.

At the same time, as discussed above, the mafia and *camorra* still exert tremendous economic leverage in wide areas of the South where economic development remains elusive. Symbolic of such leverage is the protest, coinciding with the opening of the anti-mafia trial in February 1986, of a group of Palermo workers who had been employed by a firm that had monopolized contracts for street and sewer maintenance in the city since 1938, only to lose them in the wake of anti-mafia investigations. The workers blocked traffic in front of the City Hall, brandishing placards with the following slogans: "We want the mafia;" "With the mafia there is work; without it, no." In a situation where the application of the Legge Rognoni-La Torre, stricter police controls, and the arrest of several hundred accused *mafiosi* have substantially impeded the flow of so-called *narcolire*, such protest reflects underlying social tensions which preoccupy local administrators. In response, the mayor of Palermo emphasized that, without alternative sources of public investment and economic development to replace the jobs provided by the mafia, the struggle against the mafia could not succeed (*La Repubblica*, February 1 and 14, 1986).

The problem is more complex than this, however. The problem of the South during the postwar period has not been the absence of state resources and state-sponsored development programs, but rather the ways in which those resources have been used. Beginning in the 1950s, the southern economy became profoundly intertwined with and dependent upon the resources of the state and the political power of those parties and politicians who controlled key ministries or regional assessorships. An "assisted economy" was created, in which economic success depends less on the market than on political connections. Public resources in the form of subsidies, tax breaks, contracts, and the like were distributed on the basis of political rather then economic rationality, entrepreneurship was geared to speculative gain rather than to long-term productive investment, and autonomous, self-sustaining development became an ever more distant and elusive goal.[44] In this situation, mafia and *camorra*, given their political connections, have inserted themselves with relative ease and, with their peculiar competitive advantages, have blocked the emergence of legitimate entrepreneurial forces or have compelled them, in order to compete, to resort to mafia methods themselves. Thus the call for a renewed flow of resources from the center, while a necessary

48

correction to the sharp decline in public investment in the South since the mid-1970s, is in itself no guarantee of an alternative to the current economy permeated by the mafia. Without a drastic change in the relationship between the economy and the political system in the South, it is doubtful that a "healthy" entrepreneurship in the South, be it public or private, will be able to assert itself.

This brings one back to the heart of the problem and the heart ✓ of any solution—the relationship between the mafia and politics. More than the enactment of special laws (such as those of the late 1970s against left-wing terrorism), what is necessary to defeat the mafia is the political will to apply existing laws and to rally the full weight of the state behind those police officers and magistrates exposed in the front line of the struggle against the mafia. It is the absence of that unanimous and unambiguous political will which is the most striking difference between the battle against the mafia and the successful campaign against the Red Brigades in the late 1970s and early 1980s. This difference was clearly perceived by General Dalla Chiesa, who had led the campaign against left-wing terrorism before being sent to Palermo to head the struggle against the mafia. In the struggle against terrorism, Dalla Chiesa had felt secure in the full support of the state apparatus, the political parties and public opinion. On the contrary, he lamented, in the struggle against the mafia he felt himself increasingly confronted with indifference, if not hostility, on the part of precisely those political and institutional forces whose function it should be to defend law and order and democratic institutions.[45] The situation ✓ in which he found himself during the four months he spent in Palermo, like that of the handful of dedicated police and magistrates who preceded and followed him, is brutally summarized in the following statement made by Dalla Chiesa shortly before his assassination:

> I believe I have understood the new rules of the game. A person in a position of power can be killed when this fatal combination of circumstances occurs: he has become too dangerous, but at the same time he can be eliminated because he is isolated (*La Repubblica*, August 10, 1982; cited in Dalla Chiesa 228).

Similar accusations of isolation, obstructionism, and lack of material support have been voiced repeatedly by Dalla Chiesa's colleagues in the police forces and the magistrature in Palermo, public servants who have attempted to fill with their own courage and dedication—all too often at the cost of their lives—the vacuum left by the state and the political parties. These men have denounced an erosion in the climate of popular consensus and support which surrounded them in the first months after the death of General Dalla Chiesa and a lapse into indifference or resignation among large sectors of public opinion as well as the political elite. In more concrete terms, they lament the failure to address chronic inadequacies in the number and quality of police and judicial personnel, in the availability of modern equipment (e.g., a computerized data bank), and in coordination of efforts among the different sectors of the police and the judiciary.[46] Finally, the judges themselves have come under increasing fire on charges of "political protagonism", providing insufficient guarantees of the rights of defendants, and relying excessively on the testimony of informants like the former Palermo boss, Tommaso Buscetta.

The absence of the political will and a political strategy to confront the problem of the mafia head on is demonstrated as well by the indifference with which the documentation and the recommendations produced by the Antimafia Commission of the Italian Parliament during thirteen years of activity (1963-1976) were received. Although both reports of the Commission (1972 and 1976) were unanimously approved by the members of the Commission representing the parties of the government majority, no action was taken on any of their recommendations until after the deaths of Pio La Torre (Communist deputy, member of the Antimafia Commission, and author of the legislation which would subsequently bear his name) and Carlo Alberto Dalla Chiesa in 1982. While the materials made public by the Antimafia Commission provide copious documentation of the relationships with the mafia of noted Sicilian politicians and entrepreneurs like Vito Ciancimino and Antonino and Ignazio Salvo, the political and economic power of Ciancimino and the Salvos, both pillars of the DC in Sicily, placed them in the ranks of the "untouchables" for yet another decade. Only in the changed political climate following the death of Dalla Chiesa did they finally become the objects of judicial investigation and punitive measures. But the mafia had already profited by the years of inattention following the repression of the 1960s to reorganize and capture a leading position in the international drug trade, which enabled it to mount the much more dangerous challenge it posed in the 1980s.

As has been demonstrated throughout this monograph, the mafia is not a cancer which has attacked an essentially healthy social and political body, but rather an integral part of the Italian political system. In the words of Eugenio Scalfari, in an editorial in the daily newspaper *La Repubblica*, "What is at stake is no longer... only the destiny of a region suffocated by a malignant and parasitical plant. What is at stake is the very existence of the democratic state, in Palermo, as in Rome and in Milan" (*La Repubblica*, September 6, 1982). The keys to understanding the capacity of the mafia to penetrate the Italian state lie in three distinct but interrelated spheres—the crisis of formal democratic institutions, the nature of the party system and the occupation of the state apparatus by the political parties, and the relationship between the state and the individual citizen.

In the institutional sphere, formal institutions at both the national and local levels have proven increasingly incapable of formulating coherent and effective policies in response to the social, economic, and political crises which have afflicted Italy since the late 1960s. In the vacuum left by institutional paralysis various forms of informal or "occult" power—e.g., the mafia, the P2, the secret services—have found a fertile terrain. But while the power of the mafia has penetrated to such high levels of the national political and financial systems that it constitutes a threat, if not to the survival, at least to the substance of democratic institutions, the bonds linking the mafia to its bases of popular support remain to a large extent territorial. These territorial bonds are in turn sustained by the intimate relationship between the mafia and regional and local administrations. Paradoxically, a "democratic" reform like the decentralization of the Italian state has in certain areas of the South come to constitute instead a major source of political and economic gain for the mafia. The Sicilian Region is but the most glaring example of the vast discretionary powers of single assessors and high-level civil servants and the absence of any system of effective accounting or control over the ways in which

51

public monies are spent. In response to the infiltration of local and regional government by mafia interests, the mayor of Palermo went so far as to appeal to the national government to take control of the awarding of public contracts for massive new investments slated for the city and to appoint 20,000 "super-bureaucrats" to oversee the projects (*Boston Globe*, May 29, 1988).

The paralysis of the decision-making and administrative capabilities of the Italian state has its roots in turn in the party system. The political parties have colonized the state, the institutions of which have been transformed from instruments for the enactment and implementation of policies to confront the problems of a rapidly changing society into centers of power and patronage to reinforce the political fortunes of parties, factions, and individual politicians.[47] As the state penetrated ever further into the fabric of Italian society and economy in the postwar period, and as the state apparatus itself became increasingly politicized, infiltration of the political parties became the *via maestra* to gain access to key resources and levers of power. In return for its ability to provide votes and funds to both parties and individual candidates (given the importance of the personal preference vote), the mafia received privileged access to important centers of economic power and channels of public spending.

The mafia as a criminal phenomenon sinks its roots and finds sustenance in a diffuse "*mentalita mafiosa*" which extends far beyond the *cosche* themselves and the traditional subcultural values of certain parts of the South. Where the state is conceived primarily as a vehicle for personal and factional interests, there is a blurring of the lines between public and private and between legitimate and illegitimate forms of political power and influence. The mafia is the logical extension and the ultimate degeneration of a pervasive culture of clientelism, favoritism, and the appropriation of public resources for private gain which permeates the Italian political system and large sectors of Italian society. In the 1870s Franchetti and Sonnino observed that the mafia flourished where the concept of the rule of law was subordinate to the bonds of personal obligation and the affirmation of personal might. A century later, General Dalla Chiesa launched the same accusation in even more brutal terms: "So long as a party card continues to count for more than the state, we will never win the battle" (Dalla

Chiesa 50). What has changed since the 1870s is that what was to a large extent a regional problem (albeit even then with national ramifications) has now infected the entire political system by means of precisely those "modern" political developments—the construction of a far-reaching system of DC power and the expansion of the welfare state—which integrated the postwar South ever more firmly into the national state.

In the last analysis, then, the key to defeating the mafia lies in a profound transformation of the relationship between the Italian state and its citizens—a cultural as well as a political revolution. What is necessary is to restore the legitimacy and credibility of democratic institutions, seriously undermined, especially in the South, by clientelism, corruption, and the dysfunctions of a byzantine bureaucracy where even the most basic public services are available only through the intercession of a powerful protector. This means guaranteeing the legality and transparency of public life, providing public services with efficiency and impartiality, and instituting mechanisms of inspection and control that would limit the vast discretionality which currently exists and thereby reduce the margins for favoritism, clientelistic maneuvers, and corruption. Here again, General Dalla Chiesa (paraphrasing his predecessor by half a century, the Fascist Prefect Mori) clearly perceived the roots of the problem in the few months he spent in Palermo:

> I have understood something, very simple but perhaps decisive. A large part of the protection and the privileges for which citizens pay the mafia dearly are nothing but their elementary rights. Let us assure citizens of these rights, let us take this power away from the mafia, and we will turn its dependents into our allies (*La Repubblica*, August 10, 1982; cited in Dalla Chiesa 230).

Such reforms require first and foremost, however, a profound transformation of the political parties themselves and of the methods by which they attempt to attain and to maintain power. But the paradox of this solution lies in the fact that the initiative for any reform of public institutions and any moralization of public life must come from precisely those political actors which are

53

among the prime causes of the degeneration. The intertwining of the mafia with politics is the ultimate source of its strength and must be confronted with lucidity and determination if the mafia is ever to be defeated. As the Liberal deputy Napoleone Colajanni warned at the turn of the century,

> To combat and destroy the kingdom of the mafia, it is necessary, it is indispensable, that the Italian government cease to be the *king of the mafia*! But the government has acquired too great a taste for the exercise of this dishonest and illicit authority; it is too practiced and hardened in its misdeeds. Have we come to a point where we can no longer hope for the cessation of the function without the destruction of the organism? (Colajanni 110)

ENDNOTES

1. No in-depth scholarly studies have yet appeared on the *camorra*. For an analysis of the conditions under which the Calabrian *'ndrangheta* emerged, see Arlacchi 1983: 67-121.

2. For a detailed analysis of honor, kinship, and instrumental friendship in traditional Sicilian culture, see Schneider and Schneider, 86-102; and Catanzaro 1985: 36-41.

3. This view of the mafia is most fully elaborated in Hess, 107-172.

4. A good summary of the competing interpretations of mafia structure can be found in Catanzaro 1986b: 92-98). The argument about the continuing "confederal" structure of the mafia is made both by Catanzaro and by Chinnici and Santino, 181-183.

5. On the origins of the mafia in the breakdown of feudalism, see Schneider and Schneider; Blok; and Catanzaro (1985). Catanzaro's 1985 article constitutes one portion of his recent major work in Italian on the origins and evolution of the mafia (Catanzaro, 1988).

6. Although feudalism in Sicily was formally abolished in 1812 under pressure from the British occupying forces, vestiges of feudalism persisted well into the 20th century. For a detailed discussion of the British occupation of Sicily and the Bourbon reforms of the first half of the 19th century, see Mack Smith 343-369. The impact of feudalism is underscored by data indicating that, in the first half of the 19th century, feudal estates accounted for about 90% of the land in Western Sicily (Catanzaro 1988: 88).

7. The expression is that of Blok (53-57). Although the Schneiders use a different term, "broker capitalism," they are referring to the same concept (Schneider and Schneider).

8. For a detailed discussion of "rural entrepreneurship" in 19th and early 20th century Sicily, see Schneider and Schneider 69-72.

9. Arlacchi, for example, argues that in a feudal system with strict baronial control over the *latifondo*, there is no space for the mafia (Arlacchi 1983: 123-198).

10. These functions are discussed at greater length in Arlacchi 1986: 20-54; Catanzaro 1988: 27-44, 116-138; and Hess 173-209.

11. The electorate consisted of fewer than 500,000 voters (1.9% of the population) in 1861, was increased to 2 million voters (6.9% of the population) in 1882, and universal male suffrage (8.5 million voters) was introduced in 1913.

12. In 1946, despite the abolition of feudalism, about 50% of agricultural land in Sicily was still held by 1% of the population (Mack Smith 532).

13. For a detailed account of the Sicilian Separatist movement and its relationship to the mafia, see Finkelstein; Marino; and Renda 1987: 46-77.

14. For a detailed account of the case of Salvador Giuliano, one of the great political scandals of the postwar period in Italy, see Antimafia Commission 1972, Vol. 2: 983-1031. Journalistic versions of these events can be found in Pantaleone 130-155; and Servadio 119-140.

15. Approximately 40 peasant leaders and trade-union organizers were killed in the period 1945-1948 alone. A complete list of the victims of the mafia during this period can be found in the 1976 report of the Antimafia Commission of the Italian Parliament (Antimafia Commission 1976: 154).

16. The entire first volume of Franchetti and Sonnino's *Inchiesta in Sicilia* constitutes a detailed documentation and denunciation of the clientelism and corruption which characterized public administration in Sicily fifteen years after Italian unification. Another important source denouncing the interpenetration of the mafia and politics in pre-Fascist Italy is Colajanni (1971).

17. The mafia's ties to national power were intensified after 1876, when control of the government passed to the Sinistra and leading Sicilian politicians, until then in the opposition, were brought into positions of national power.

18. This article in English is a condensed version of Catanzaro's major recent work on the mafia, the central thesis of which is this argument about "social hybridization" (Catanzaro 1988).

19. Probably the best depiction of the social and political webs of complicity surrounding the mafia is to be found in the Sicilian writer Leonardo Sciascia's novel, *The Day of the Owl* (Sciascia 1983).

20. For an in-depth analysis of the relationship between the mafia and the Fascist state, see Duggan (1989).

21. There is no conclusive documentation of the relationship between the Allied occupation forces and the mafia. These ties are alluded to, however, in the reports of both the U.S. Senate Committee on Organized Crime (Kefauver, 1968) and of the Antimafia Commission of the Italian Parliament (Antimafia Commission 1976: 115-118); other sources on this period include Renda 1987: 77-98; Pantaleone 44-58; and Servadio 79-94.

22. For a more detailed analysis of the evolution of the DC in the South from the end of the war until the mid-1950s, see Chubb 55-77.

23. For a detailed account of the collusion between the mafia and the city government of Palermo, see Antimafia Commission 1972, Vol. 1: 873-952; and Chubb 128-158.

24. For an analysis of the transformation of the DC in the South into a political machine and the functioning of that machine at the local level, see Allum; Caciagli et al.; and Chubb.

25. Although no exact data exist to document the presence of *mafiosi* or members of their families inside the regional bureaucracy, an indicator of such a presence is the over-representation of the "mafia" provinces of Western Sicily. Although the population of western Sicily is about 50% of the regional total, these provinces account for 73.2% of regional personnel (Arlacchi 1986: 73; Catanzaro 1988: 182).

26. An excellent example of the mixture of archaic and modern methods can be seen in the kidnapping of Paul Getty, Jr., in 1973. The ransom money of a billion lire paid to liberate Getty, whose ear was cut off and sent to his family, was utilized by the *mafiosi* of Gioia Tauro to finance the acquisition of the equipment necessary to execute the contracts for the industrial port.

27. Income per capita in the South, which increased from 54% of that of the Center-North in 1951 to 62.3% in 1971, had declined to 60.3% in 1985 (SVIMEZ 1986: 36). Unemployment increased steadily in the South throughout the 1980s, reaching 16.4% in 1985, as opposed to 10.5% in the Center-North. Within the South, the three regions most afflicted by the mafia (Sicily, Campania, and Calabria) had the highest unemployment rates—15.6%, 17.6%, and 18.7% respectively (SVIMEZ 1986: 25). Finally, in terms of an index of industrialization based on industrial employment and production per capita, Sicily and Calabria are the least industrialized regions in the South (30 and 18 respectively given 100 for the Center-North), and their level of industrialization has actually declined since 1970 (SVIMEZ 1985: 137).

28. The Palermo magistrate Rocco Chinnici, subsequently assassinated by the mafia, estimated that 60-70% of the funds distributed by the regional assessor of agriculture ended up in the hands of the mafia (*La Repubblica*, August 2, 1983).

29. The data on the expansion of the banking system are taken from a study prepared by the Centro Ricerche Economiche Angelo Curella of the Banca Popolare Sant'Angelo in Palermo. A more detailed statistical analysis of the evolution of the banking system in Sicily may be found in Cusimano 109-116. Some observers have criticized the interpretation of this data as an indicator of mafia penetration of the banking system, arguing that the tremendous expansion of the banking system in Sicily was necessary in order to overcome the almost total monopoly held by major national banks in the 1950s and to make the banking system more competitive and more equitably distributed with respect to territory and population (e.g., Busetta 13-22). While there is clearly some basis to these observations, the magnitude of the increase and the consequent fragmentation of the banking system have constituted a fertile terrain for the recycling of illicit gains, as indicated by the investigations carried out under the aegis of the Rognoni-La Torre law, which for the first time allowed the police and the magistrature access to records of financial transactions.

30. For a more detailed discussion of the linkages between the mafia and bankers like Sindona and Calvi, see Chubb and Vannicelli.

31. In addition to the illicit profits which are recycled into legitimate business enterprises, a substantial portion find their way back into the drug trade, into the Third World arms traffic, or into secret bank accounts and overseas fiscal havens.

32. Estimates of the total import of the "criminal economy" in Italy are by their very nature highly approximate. Such estimates vary from 25,000 billion lire (about 5% of GNP) to 100,000 billion lire (about 20% of GNP). Estimates of the total number of individuals employed in illicit activities oscillate between 500,000 and 1,000,000 (2.5%-5% of the labor force); see Arlacchi (1985) and Martinoli (1985). A leading magistrate estimated the incidence of the mafia in the Sicilian economy to be as high as 25% (Rocco Chinnici, *La Repubblica*, August 2, 1983).

33. The figures on labor force participation refer to the Census category "popolazione attiva in condizione professionale." They include the employed and those unemployed due to the loss of a prior job, but exclude young people in search of a first job.

34. Emblematic of such shared interests are individuals like Michele Sindona, Antonino and Ignazio Salvo, and Vito Ciancimino, former mayor of Palermo and until recently a major figure in the Christian Democratic Party in Sicily. The arrests of Ciancimino and the Salvos in December 1984 were seen as major turning points in the effort to strike at the heretofore untouchable "third level" of mafia power (the networks of political-financial support). However, there is widespread feeling that these local power brokers served as scapegoats to forestall action against more highly placed political figures. For example, Salvo Lima, head of the Andreotti faction of the DC in Sicily, ex-parliamentary deputy, and currently a member of the European Parliament, was mentioned 149 times in the documentation of the Antimafia Commission, yet continues his political career untroubled by either party or judicial sanctions. For a more detailed account of the careers of Ciancimino and Lima, see Chubb 67-71, 77-80, 133-138, 144-151.

35. On mafia connections with Sindona, the P2, right-wing terrorism, and the secret services, see Chubb and Vannicelli, as well as the judicial documents on the Sindona case (*Gli atti d'accusa dei giudici di Milano*); the minority report of the parliamentary commission which investigated the P2 (Teodori); and Turone.

36. Chinnici and Santino provide a detailed analysis of homicides in Palermo during both the 1960-1966 and 1978-1984 periods. During the 1979-1984 period a similar war for supremacy broke out among the various families of the Neapolitan *camorra*, provoking 987 deaths throughout the region of Campania (Antimafia Commission 1985: 58). At the peak of the mafia war in 1981-1983 the homicide rate in the city of Palermo reached levels of 21.6-30.2/100,000 as opposed to a rate of 4.2-4.4/100,000 for all of Italy (Chinnici and Santino 15-16).

37. For a detailed account of the controversy over the conferral of special powers on the General, see the book by his son (Dalla Chiesa, 1984).

38. Pio La Torre, a Communist deputy and the party's regional secretary in Sicily, introduced the legislation in March 1980; the legislation would subsequently carry both his name and that of the Christian Democratic Minister of the Interior when the legislation was enacted. La Torre was himself assassinated by the mafia on May Day in 1982. While no arrests have yet been made, most observers feel that he was murdered precisely because of his outspoken support for such tough new legislative measures against the "financial" mafia, as well as his denunciation of mafia infiltration in the building of the NATO base in Comiso in eastern Sicily.

39. Typical of such resistance is the statement by the Christian Democratic mayor of Palermo, Nello Martellucci (*La Nazione* [Florence], April 8, 1982).

40. For a detailed statistical analysis of the results of the Rognoni-La Torre law in its first two years, see Cazzola, Lanza, and Roccuzzo. See also the series of articles in the volume edited by Fiandaca and Costantino.

41. For a summary of the documentation produced by the Palermo magistrates, see Stajano.

42. The impact which the Palermo sentences made on public opinion was seriously undermined by the acquittal of 20 major mafia bosses on grounds of insufficient evidence in the third maxi-trial in April 1989. These high-level bosses had been tried for their membership in the so-called Commission, accused of ordering seven murders during the 1979-1984 mafia war. Their acquittals shed doubt on the very concept of a unified mafia hierarchy, as well as on the credibility of mafia informants like Tommaso Buscetta. At the conclusion of the trial, the magistrate in charge announced, "We have gone back to year one in the struggle against the mafia" (*Corriere della Sera*, April 17, 1989).

43. For a unique collection of documents of local Church officials in Sicily, Calabria, and Campania dealing with the question of the mafia, see *Segno* (Palermo), nos. 34-35 (July-October 1982), pp. 149-188.

44. For an in-depth analysis of the relationship between politics and entrepreneurship in the South, see Catanzaro (1979).

45. See Dalla Chiesa, in particular the General's letter to then Prime Minister, Giovanni Spadolini (pp. 32-33).

46. The most forceful of such denunciations have been made in lengthy interviews to the daily press by the best known of the Palermo magistrates, Giovanni Falcone (*La Repubblica*, April 13, 1985, and November 4, 1986). In August 1988, Falcone, citing "omissions and inertia," as well as a "defamatory campaign," requested a transfer, and most members of his nine-man team have threatened to leave if he does. Described as "the greatest living archive on the mafia," and credited with having revolutionized anti-mafia investigative methods, Falcone has been so central to the judicial

campaign against the mafia that observers fear his departure could set efforts back by at least a decade (*Boston Globe*, August 7, 1988).

47. For an excellent analysis of the workings of the Italian political system, see Spotts and Wieser, especially Chapters 6 and 7. A fuller argument as to the connections between scandals and corruption and the nature of the Italian party system can be found in Chubb and Vannicelli.

Bibliography

Allum, Percy (1973) *Politics and Society in Post-War Naples* (Cambridge: Cambridge University Press).

Antimafia Commission (1972) *Testo integrale della relazione della commissione parlamentare d'inchiesta sul fenomeno della mafia* (Rome: Cooperativa Scrittori).

____. (1976) *Commissione parlamentare d'inchiesta sul fenomeno della mafia in Sicilia, Relazione conclusiva* (Rome: Senato della Repubblica).

____. (1985) *Commissione parlamentare sul fenomeno della mafia, Relazione di maggioranza* (Rome: Camera dei Deputati/Senato della Repubblica).

Arlacchi, Pino (1983) *Mafia, Peasants and Great Estates* (New York: Cambridge University Press).

Arlacchi, Pino (1985) "La grande holding della criminalita," *La Repubblica* (December 15, 1985).

____. (1986) *Mafia Business: The Mafia Ethic and the Spirit of Capitalism* (London: Verso).

Blok, Anton (1974) *The Mafia of a Sicilian Village, 1860-1960: A Study of Violent Peasant Entrepreneurs* (New York: Harper and Row).

Busetta, Pietro M. (1983) "Evoluzione dei tassi: Il caso Sicilia," *Delta 3* [a publication of the Cassa di Risparmio di Puglia], March-April, pp. 13-22.

Caciagli, Mario et al. (1977) *Democrazia Cristiana e potere nel Mezzogiorno* (Florence: Guaraldi).

Catanzaro, Raimondo (1979) *L'imprenditore assistito* (Bologna: Il Mulino).

____. (1985) "Enforcers, entrepreneurs, and survivors: How the *mafia* has adapted to change," *The British Journal of Sociology*, Vol. 36, n. 1 (March), pp. 34-57.

_____. (1986a) "Impresa mafiosa, economia e sistemi di regolazione sociale: Appunti sul caso siciliano," in G. Fiandaca and S Costantino, eds., *La legge antimafia tre anni dopo* (Milan: France Angeli), pp. 177-193.

_____. (1986b) "The mafia," in Robert Leonardi and Raffaella Y. Nanetti eds., *Italian Politics: A Review, Volume 1* (London and Wolfeboro N.H.: Frances Pinter), pp. 87-101.

_____. (1988) *L'impresa come delitto: Storia sociale della mafia* (Padua Liviana).

Cazzola, Franco, Rosario Lanza, and Antonio Roccuzzo (1985 "L'applicazione della Legge Rognoni-LaTorre nelle relazion dell'Alto Commissario per la lotta contro la mafia" (Catania Istituto Gramsci Siciliano/Osservatorio sulla mafi; [mimeograph]).

Chinnici, Giorgio, and Umberto Santino (1986) *L'omicidio a Palermo provincia negli anni 1960-1966 e 1978-1984* (Palermo: Universit; di Palermo).

Chubb, Judith (1982) *Patronage, Power and Poverty in Southern Ital* (New York: Cambridge Univeristy Press).

_____. and Maurizio Vannicelli (1988) "Italy: A Web of Scandals in Flawed Democracy," in Andrei Markovits and Mark Silversteir eds., *The Politics of Scandal* (New York: Holmes and Meier).

Colajanni, Napoleone (1971) *Nel regno della mafia* (Palermo: Renz; Mazzone [original edition 1900]).

Cusimano, Gaetano (1985) "The Banking System and Economic Growt in Sicily," *Journal of Regional Policy* (January-March), pp. 10S 116.

Dalla Chiesa, Nando (1984) *Delitto imperfetto* (Milan: Mondadori).

Dolci, Danilo (1964) *Waste* (New York: Monthly Review Press).

Duggan, Christopher (1989) *Fascism and the Mafia* (New Haven: Yal University Press).

Fiandaca, G. and S. Costantino, eds. (1986)*La legge antimafia tre ann dopo* (Milan: Franco Angeli).

Finkelstein, Monte S. (1985) "Sicilian Separatism, the Mafia, and the Origins of Sicilian Autonomy, 1943-1946" (Unpublished paper).

Franchetti, Leopoldo and Sidney Sonnino (1974) "Condizioni politiche e amministrative della Sicilia," *Inchiesta in Sicilia, Vol. 1* (Florence: Vallecchi [original edition 1876]).

Gambetta, Diego (1988) "Fragments of an economic theory of the mafia," *Archives europeenes de sociologie*, Vol. 29, pp. 127-145.

____. (1986) *Gli atti d'accusa dei giudici di Milano* (Rome: Editori Riuniti).

Hess, Henner (1973) *Mafia* (Bari: Laterza).

Kefauver, Estes (1968) *Crime in America* (Westport, Conn.: Greenwood [original edition 1951]).

Lupo, Salvatore (1988) "'Il tenebroso sodalizio': Un rapporto sulla mafia palermitana di fine ottocento," *Studi Storici*, n. 2, pp. 463-489.

Lyttleton, Adrian (1989) "Breaking a code of honour," *Times Literary Supplement* (March 3-9), pp. 211-213.

Mack Smith, Denis (1968) *A History of Sicily: Modern Sicily After 1713* (New York: Viking).

Mangiameli, Rosario (1984) "Gabellotti e notabili nella Sicilia dell'interno," *Italia contemporanea*, n. 156 (September), pp. 55-67.

Marino, Giuseppe Carlo (1979) *Storia del separatismo siciliano* (Rome: Editori Riuniti).

Martinoli, Gino (1985) "Dimensioni economiche dell'illecito in Italia," in *CENSIS, Quindicinale di note e commenti*, n. 4 (April).

Pantaleone, Michele (1962) *Mafia e politica* (Turin: Einaudi).

Pitre, Giuseppe (1889) *Usi e costumi, credenze e pregiudizi del popolo siciliano, Vol. 2* (Palermo).

Renda, Francesco (1983) "La mafia nel secondo dopoguerra: Una interpretazione storiografica," in *Mafia e potere* [proceedings of an international conference held at the University of Messina, October 14-23, 1981], Vol. 2 (Soveria Mannelli: Rubbettino).

____. (1985) "Mafia e politica," in Camillo Pantaleone, ed., *Mafia ieri e oggi* (Palermo: Istituto Gramsci Siciliano).

____. (1987) *Storia della Sicilia dal 1860 al 1970, Vol. 3* (Palermo: Sellerio Editore).

Sabetti, Filippo (1984) *Political Authority in a Sicilian Village* (New Brunswick, N.J.: Rutgers University Press).

Santino, Umberto (1982) "La conquista di Bisanzio: borghesia mafiosa e Stato dopo il delitto Dalla Chiesa," *Segno* (Palermo), nos. 34-35 (July-October), pp. 11-34.

Schneider, Jane and Peter (1976) *Culture and Political Economy in Western Sicily* (New York: Academic Press).

Sciascia, Leonardo (1983) *The Day of the Owl* (Boston: Godine).

Servadio, Gaia (1976) *Mafioso* (New York: Dell).

Spotts, Frederic and Theodor Wieser (1986) *Italy: A Difficult Democracy* (Cambridge and New York: Cambridge University Press).

Stajano, Corrado, ed. (1986) *Mafia: L'atto d'accusa dei giudici di Palermo* (Rome: Editori Riuniti).

SVIMEZ (1985) *Rapporto 1985 sull'economia del Mezzogiorno* (Rome: SVIMEZ).

____. (1986) *Rapporto 1986 sull'economia del Mezzogiorno* (Rome: SVIMEZ).

Tarrow, Sidney (1967) *Peasant Communism in Southern Italy* (New Haven: Yale University Press).

Teodori, Massimo (1981) *P2: La controstoria* (Milan: SugarCo).

Turone, Sergio (1985) *Partiti e mafia dalla P2 alla droga* (Bari: Laterza).

Villari, Pasquale (1979) *Le lettere meridionali e altri scritti sulla questione sociale in Italia* (Naples: Guida [original edition 1878]).